4

OLD TESTAMENT

COLLEGEVILLE BIBLE COMMENTARY

LEVITICUS

Wayne A. Turner

THE LITURGICAL PRESS

Collegeville, Minnesota

ABBREVIATIONS

Gen—Genesis
Exod—Exodus
Lev—Leviticus
Num—Numbers
Deut—Deuteronomy
Josh—Joshua
Judg—Judges
Ruth—Ruth
1 Sam—1 Samuel
2 Sam—2 Samuel
1 Kgs—1 Kings
2 Kgs—2 Kings
1 Chr—1 Chronicles
2 Chr—2 Chronicles
Ezra—Ezra
Neh—Nehemiah
Tob—Tobit
Jdt—Judith
Esth—Esther
1 Macc—1 Maccabees
2 Macc—2 Maccabees
Job—Job
Ps(s)—Psalm(s)
Prov—Proverbs

Eccl—Ecclesiastes
Song—Song of Songs
Wis—Wisdom
Sir—Sirach
Isa—Isaiah
Jer—Jeremiah
Lam—Lamentations
Bar—Baruch
Ezek—Ezekiel
Dan—Daniel
Hos—Hosea
Joel—Joel
Amos—Amos
Obad—Obadiah
Jonah—Jonah
Mic—Micah
Nah—Nahum
Hab—Habakkuk
Zeph—Zephaniah
Hag—Haggai
Zech—Zechariah
Mal—Malachi
Matt—Matthew
Mark—Mark
Luke—Luke

John—John
Acts—Acts
Rom—Romans
1 Cor—1 Corinthians
2 Cor—2 Corinthians
Gal—Galatians
Eph—Ephesians
Phil—Philippians
Col—Colossians
1 Thess—1 Thessalonians
2 Thess—2 Thessalonians
1 Tim—1 Timothy
2 Tim—2 Timothy
Titus—Titus
Phlm—Philemon
Heb—Hebrews
Jas—James
1 Pet—1 Peter
2 Pet—2 Peter
1 John—1 John
2 John—2 John
3 John—3 John
Jude—Jude
Rev—Revelation

Nihil obstat: Robert C. Harren, J.C.L., *Censor deputatus.*

Imprimatur: ✝ George H. Speltz, D.D., Bishop of St. Cloud. January 14, 1985.

ISBN 0-8146-1372-1 (volume 4 O.T.); ISBN 0-8146-1394-2 (22-volume set O.T.)

Library of Congress Cataloging in Publication Data

Turner, Wayne A., 1925–
    Leviticus.

    Collegeville Bible commentary. Old Testament ; 4)
    Includes the complete text of Leviticus.
    1. Bible. O.T. Leviticus—Commentaries. I. Bible.
O.T. Leviticus. English. New American. 1985.
II. Title. III. Series.
BS1225.3.T87 1985   222'.13077   85-216
ISBN 0-8146-1372-1

Cover: A Jewish boy holds the Torah by the Sabbath table. *Photo by Betty Hurwich Zoss.*

CONTENTS

Introduction   5

Text and Commentary*   15

   I. Ritual of Sacrifices (1–7)   15

     Chapters 1, 2, 3   Holocaust, Cereal and Peace Offerings   15

     4, 5   Sin Offerings and Special Cases   22

     6, 7   Further Ritual and Prohibition of Blood, Fat   26

   II. Ceremony of Ordination (8–10)   29

     Chapters 8, 9, 10   Ordination, Octave and Conduct of Priest   30

   III. Laws Regarding Legal Purity (11–16)   35

     Chapters 11, 12   Clean and Unclean Food   36

     13, 14   Leprosy and Its Purification   40

     15   Personal Uncleanness   48

     16   The Day of Atonement   49

   IV. Code of Legal Holiness (17–26)   54

     Chapters 17, 18   Sacredness of Blood and Sex   54

     19, 20   Various Rules of Conduct and Penalties   59

     21, 22   Sanctity of Priest and Victim   67

     23   Holy Days   69

     24   Sanctuary Light, Showbread, Blasphemy   72

     25   Sabbatical, Jubilee Years, Property Redeemed   74

     26   Obedience and Disobedience   78

   V. Redemption of Offerings (27)   81

     Chapter 27   Votive Offerings   81

Review Aids and Discussion Topics   86

---

*Each subdivision is a reading-session (1, 2, and 3 are to be read together and then 4 and 5). Begin to read at Part IV (17–26) and then come back to Part I. Read the text first, then the commentary. Reread the text and then go on to the next section.

The Book of Leviticus

Introduction

This is a book about holiness. Known also as the third book of Moses, the Book of Leviticus is one volume in the five-volume work called the Pentateuch. The term Torah, which usually means law, but more exactly is teaching, instruction, or direction, refers to the message of this book. Even though we customarily refer to Leviticus as a book, it is better to call it one chapter in the whole story of the Torah. This chapter is about a holy God and a people called to be holy.

1. Holiness means wholeness

To understand this chapter in the Torah story we need to consider "wholeness" as one meaning of holiness. This is more than a play on words and is necessary to understand the Book of Leviticus. Wholeness, in a sense, describes the life of God. More precisely, wholeness describes our lives when they reflect the life of God.

The biblical meaning of holiness includes not only the mystery of God but also the creature's response to that mystery. "Be holy, for I, the Lord, your God, am holy" (11:44-45; 19:2; 20:7, 26). The root of the word holy means "to cut off, separate," referring to the separation of the holy from the profane (unholy). "Holy" refers to persons, places, or things approached or touched only under certain conditions of ritual purity.

"Wholeness" describes particularly the response of the people to the command "Be holy, for I, the Lord, am holy." For, while there is a certain wholeness to the idea of oneness, God alone resides in absolute oneness. There is also a certain oneness about wholeness, which can reflect what Genesis calls the "image and likeness of God" (1:26).

Wholeness, unlike oneness, has parts or components. It is in the proper ordering of the parts of life that wholeness comes about and serves the cause of holiness. For example, a jigsaw puzzle must be put together in a particular order. If even one piece is left over, the puzzle lacks wholeness and oneness.

As we read the Book of Leviticus, we must keep in mind that everything fits together in a proper order. This serves the wholeness that reflects the oneness of God who called the people to be holy. The simple order of obe-

dience, ritual purity, and holiness is as valid today as when first presented by the Priestly writers. True obedience plants the seed of an authentic ritual that purifies and prepares for the life of holiness. Once this simple lesson-plan was recognized, the Levitical material took its shape. Then this book acted as the key piece for the Pentateuch and became the third book of Moses. The five books formed one complete account of divine-human relationship, with Leviticus as the very heart of the Torah.

2. The titles tell the story

The Hebrew titles of the five books of Moses spell out a theme that is repeated again and again in the Bible and in life itself—God creates, identifies, and calls people from the wilderness of this life into the one, complete (holy) life that is God's. These books act as the "entrance" to the whole Bible.

In the Hebrew Bible the first significant word of each book is the title for that book. In the Pentateuch the Hebrew titles make a logical statement of the divine-human experience. *In the beginning* (Genesis) God created; these are the *names* (Exodus), *and he called* (Leviticus) Moses *in the wilderness* (Numbers) to speak these *words* (Deuteronomy). Note the place of Leviticus; the *names* (Exodus) of those led out of slavery needed direction to follow their calling as a "kingdom of priests and a holy nation" (19:6), especially *in the wilderness* (Numbers).

When reading Leviticus keep in mind the "guideline character" of this chapter in the one story that makes up the Pentateuch.

3. The title

The title in Hebrew is one word meaning "and he called." Today the common title is the Latinized Greek name *Leviticus,* which describes activities of the Levites (priests) from the tribe of Levi. The Hebrew title points to a vocation-call in the instruction of the Torah. So when using *Leviticus,* it is well to keep in mind the Hebrew overtone of "calling" or "vocation."

This central theme of a call to holiness is found in the Code of Holiness (17-26). It possibly formed an original "manual of holiness" around which the final editors of the book gathered other priestly (Levitical) material.

4. Three codes of law (instruction) in the Pentateuch

Three such Codes of Law have been identified in the Pentateuch: the Sinai or Covenant Code, which is the oldest and found in the Book of Exodus (19-24); the Levitical Code of Holiness (Lev 17-26); and an updating of the Torah in the Deuteronomy Code (Deut 12-26). Even though these three are considered the Codes of Law, many other passages in the Pentateuch speak of legal regulations. In fact, the Levitical regulations are not only in the Book

of Leviticus but also in the second and the fourth books of Moses, Exodus and Numbers. Actually, there is more mention of the Levites elsewhere in the Pentateuch than in the Book of Leviticus. Here we concentrate on the "call to holiness."

5. Leviticus—heart of the Torah

Leviticus not only teaches holiness; the book itself is an example of holiness. The orderly arrangement is our first evidence of the presence of holiness. A simple arrangement of the material can be an important witness to holiness. Note that the matter of sacrifices (chs. 1–7) leads naturally into the subject of those who offer them (chs. 8–10) with their dispositions of legal purity (chs. 11–16) and legal holiness (chs. 17–27)—such a simple arrangement and yet filled with importance and authority calling the people to follow the Torah.

The book is something like the simple but decisive presence of the heart in the human organism. Even when its presence and precision of function are taken for granted, it continues to beat for the good of the whole organism. The material assigned to Leviticus seems to have a similar relation to the whole Torah. Leviticus is the heart of the Torah, and the beat of this heart is called the Code of Holiness (chs. 17–26).

The depth and elegance of the simple arrangement of Leviticus is revealed, first in the pulsating rhythm of the repeated "And the Lord spoke to Moses." After the vocational call of Moses in chapter 1, almost every chapter begins with this same refrain. The repetition is also a reminder of the form of a legal document with its repetition of formal phrases, details, and directions. In fact, roughly corresponding to the above four areas of arrangement, some legal-minded commentators point to underlying detailed arrangements. Some find seven sets of decalogues in each section. They say that they are patterned after the Decalogue (Ten Commandments) given on Mount Sinai. Thus, Leviticus, as the heart of the Torah, reflects the fine design of a heart and the simplicity of one of its single life-giving beats.

The commandments were now to come alive in the lives of the newly-formed people. The heart of the new priestly nation must now begin to beat and carry out the instruction to be holy (19:2). This holiness is at work in the Torah and throughout the whole Bible. "Holy" and "sacred" and other related forms are used over a thousand times, with nearly one quarter of such references in Leviticus.

St. Jerome in a letter to the cleric Paulinus affirms the holiness of the book: "In the Book of Leviticus it is easy to see that every sacrifice, yes, almost every syllable and both the garments of Aaron and the whole order of Leviticus breathe heavenly mysteries." Years later another Scripture writer,

Peter, encourages the vocational call of Leviticus: "So gird the loins of your understanding, live soberly, set all your hope on the gift to be conferred on you when Jesus Christ appears. As obedient sons, do not yield to the desires that once shaped you in your ignorance. Rather, become holy yourselves in every aspect of your conduct, after the likeness of the Holy One who called you; remember Scripture says, 'You shall be holy, for I am holy'" (1 Pet 1:13-16 quoting Lev 19:2). This same pulsating beat of holiness endures today in the vocational call of everyone.

6. The shape of Leviticus—date and authorship

Today we usually think of a book as having one or two authors and written over just a few years. However, the Bible is the history of the people of God written by many authors and editors over two thousand years. Just as we can expect many changes in the history of a people, we can expect changes in the documents that record that history. Scholars sometimes speak of a particular manuscript family when referring to various manuscripts.

We now recognize that some final editors were not just compilers, but were true authors. Editors also reshaped or added material along the way. In Leviticus the form of the material is *historical* and *legal,* dealing with the call to holiness. Much of the material, especially in the first chapters, is "liturgical," having been written and edited by Levites or priests and given the name "Priestly" (P).

The Book of Leviticus has a unique shape and fits into a larger unit of the Pentateuch. This larger unit extends from Exod 25 through Leviticus to Num 10. Every book of the Pentateuch has some sections written by P. The emphasis given by these writers and final editors focuses on the underlying need to be holy.

One gets the impression that Leviticus, though edited, was substantially preserved, rather than abbreviated, to form a synthesis of worship regulations. This might explain why the Bible reader often bypasses Leviticus with the expression "Oh, it's just a bunch of laws and regulations." This is a valid first impression, but the editors used this material to fill a need for guidance and completeness. The final editors intentionally gave a wilderness setting to Exodus, Leviticus, and Numbers. What could be more needed in the wilderness than a book on law (direction) and order?

Just as we recognize schools of writers, so we find today schools of scholars presenting various answers to dating, text, and authorship questions. For some, Moses is the author, while others hold that the book is postexilic (late fifth century B.C.E.). Yet another group stands a near-middle ground and gives a date around the eighth century B.C.E. Further, it may be that the final shape was not decided at any one of these times. Such theories

should help the reader understand the final form of a biblical book.

It is in the final editing that the whole message is conveyed. The shape of the book at the time it is born into the holy life of the Bible is the time when its divine source of life (i.e., divine inspiration) is affirmed. All the oral and written traditions, development of thought and practice, writing, editing and reediting come together in the Bible to serve the one, holy God. Leviticus witnesses this presence of God.

In considering the wilderness setting of the Book of Leviticus, somewhere a prejudice against temple worship could have influenced the shaping of the material. This prejudice could have occurred more than once. Also, the dispersion of population and distance of travel affect ritual practice. It is further possible that there were those who were convinced that Yahweh should be a pilgrim God, not having a fixed abode in this world except in the Holy of Holies of the Tabernacle, an abode that could travel with them wherever they would go, even into exile.

This commentary seeks to affirm the Book of Leviticus as it is in the Pentateuch, since this is the result of the final editing. The ancient editors presented a particular coherence for the ingathering of all the materials and traditions. Sometimes that ancient part of Leviticus, the Code of Holiness (17–26), is attributed to an author called H who is earlier than any of the Priestly writers.

7. Levitical themes

A. *Read the directions.* One regulation in everyday life simply says, "Read the directions." Sometimes it is touched with irony when someone says, "When everything else fails, read the directions!" Reading the directions is, no doubt, the first thing to do when beginning a new project. This advice could act as a meditation for reading the Book of Leviticus. In a way Leviticus serves as the directions for the whole Torah.

Leviticus gives a simple direction for life. The direction is as important and enduring as the beat and pulse of the heart is to the body. It is found in the lesson plan of obedience, purity, and holiness. The order is important. We begin with an obedience that brings about purification. This combination, in turn, conditions one for the life of holiness. So the direction for living a holy life is in Leviticus, centered around the simple directive of chapter 19, "Be holy, for I, the Lord, your God, am holy."

The Holy One of Israel (Isa 1:4) is God and God's name is Holy (Lev 22:32). The people, too, are to be holy. This is the regulation of life: "Sanctify yourselves, then, and be holy. . . . Be careful, therefore, to observe what I, the Lord, who make you holy, have prescribed" (20:7-8; *see also* 22:31-33).

B. *Israel's responsibility to its neighbors.* To understand the Book of Leviticus, we must respect the neighborhood in which Israel lived and moved. We proceed with caution from what we know to search out the unknown. Sometimes we expect a greater responsibility (ability-to-respond) on the part of Israel than we should. This is often done by including all the people of the then-known world into the circle of Israel's response to life. This approach tends to become a smothering, rather than a drawing-out experience. We need to know more about the people of that time before we transfer the biblical narrative into real life experiences and judge historical events.

The relationship of Israel with the Canaanite and other peoples into whose land they sojourned or moved is of prime importance. The discoveries at Ras Shamra (on the Mediterranean, dating from 1400 B.C.E.) and Ebla (75 miles northeast, dating from 2300 B.C.E.) shed some light on the neighbors of the people of the Bible (*see,* for example, Exod 23). However, much material is still in the stage of critical analysis and publication. The translations themselves take many years. Ras Shamra (Ugarit) was first excavated in 1929, and some parallels to Israel's language and literature both there and at Ebla (1968–1974) have been recognized.

C. *My holy name.* A more exact translation of "my holy name" is "the name of my holiness." In Hebrew "holiness" refers to a concrete reality for which the emphasis is intended. Another example, "my good day," is really "the day of my goodness." Hebrew places the emphasis where it belongs.

Another important difference is using the superlative to preserve a certain dignified identity. For "holiest," the Hebrew says "the Holy of Holies."

A third difference not to be overlooked when reading the Bible is that certain realities in Hebrew thought are not considered separate entities as they are in our Western thought. Ideas such as body and soul, blood and life, thought and action, are almost always considered the same reality. In Hebrew thought, for instance, there is no word for body. "Flesh" is used instead. Thus, "all flesh" is really every created living thing and is equivalent to "every living soul." Because blood and life are intimately associated, it is the blood of Abel that cries out to God from the soil (Gen 4:10). Nor are understanding and good apart from life itself, "Give me understanding (discernment), that I may live" (Ps 119:144). The expression "Adam knew Eve and she conceived Cain" means that they had intercourse (since there is no separation of body and soul, the action can be called a knowledge). It is sharing one's life with another in the action that truthfully (knowingly) expresses the oneness of God reflected in the man-woman creation.

Biblical thought does not really contain what we are accustomed to think of as a code of ethics. Thus, in speaking of the Torah we should avoid the Western term law. The Torah is not a system of laws. The Torah comes from

God, to teach, regulate, instruct and distinguish. "Law," in our Western thought, makes it a mere code of ethics. The Bible says, "Oh how I love your Torah, it is my meditation all the day" (see Ps 119).

D. *A common language of cult activity in the ancient Near East.* Over the centuries various reasons have been given for ritual and dietary regulations. The historian Philo and the philosopher Maimonides believed that God gave some of the commands and regulations in order to serve as a self-discipline of the appetites. Philo says that Moses forbade pork, since it is the most delicious of all meats and that self-denial would curb one's self-indulgence. He forbade flesh-eating animals and birds in order to teach one to be gentle and kind. Sometimes analogies were made between physical and spiritual. Thus, the cud-chewing animals are permitted, since they help one grow in wisdom (by chewing over and over what one has learned). And the cloven-footed animals, because they have a divided hoof, help one know how to decide between ideas. Maimonides also gives health-care as a reason for some of the regulations.

Regarding the prohibitions concerning food, we suspect that most ancient peoples used the trial-and-error method based on taste. What tasted good and did not make one sick was clean or good. What we call taboo was probably a scare tactic to keep people from being poisoned. The "good sign" encouraged people to eat properly. What were practical considerations for one people became directives based on religious beliefs for another and were handed on as traditions to succeeding generations. Much of what we call ancient myth was simply the stirrings of humans in seeking the source of life and how to survive in life. Nomadic, agricultural and, eventually, urban living, would inevitably bring change in outlook, custom, and religious practice. Just the natural change of the seasons and the struggle for food, which we sometimes refer to as acts of nature, influenced the shaping of desire, understanding, planning, and celebration of life.

We recognize a certain kind of common language used throughout the Near East in regard to religious belief and practice. Israel used this language also, but with a particular meaning and emphasis directed to the One Holy Yahweh.

When people began to settle in the land with an agrarian lifestyle and with food assured, the need to preserve a certain stability became dominant. Priests, prophets, kings, and queens established order to survive, not only as individuals, tribes, or small family groups but as nations. Thus the Bible is a two thousand-year-old record of a people establishing their identity in relation to their God and their neighbors.

We really do not know a great deal about the early development of cult and religious practice. Exegesis, which applies critical methods of study to

Scripture with the help of other sciences, especially archaeology, has helped our understanding in some measure. We know very little about the actual ritual of the sacrifice and practically nothing about the prayers or the commentary accompanying the ritual action and the dietary laws. The Book of Leviticus is a listing of ritual regulations, rather than a detailed description of actual performance. We do not have records of what was prayed, said, or sung during the discharge of the regulations.

It is in service of the Holy One then that we live our life of holiness, and our first regulation is to re-establish the order of God's creation in oneself and community. "Be holy" is the core meaning of "Seder" ("everything in proper order") in the Passover celebration that continues to this day in Jewish-Christian religious practice. The heart of the Torah still beats in the Book of Leviticus. The repeated call of Moses and the people to holiness in the pulse of the Code of Holiness is heard and answered at the Passover meal.

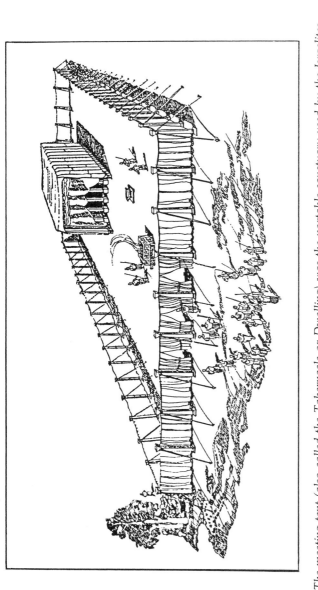

The meeting tent (also called the Tabernacle or Dwelling) was the portable sanctuary used by the Israelites during their wanderings in the desert. It is described in Exod 25–27, 35–38. It was the place of divine revelation and the center of Israel's worship and sacrifice until the time of Solomon's temple.

The meeting tent was erected in a court 150 feet long and 75 feet wide, the sides of which were covered with linen curtains. Also in the court stood the altar of burnt offerings and the bronze laver used by the priests for ritual ablutions.

The tent itself, a wooden structure 45 by 15 feet, was divided by a veil into two parts: the Holy Place and the Holy of Holies. The Holy Place contained the golden lampstand, the table of showbread, and the altar of incense. The Holy of Holies contained the ark of the covenant, which held the stone tablets of the law.

The Book of Leviticus

Text and Commentary

I: RITUAL OF SACRIFICES

1 Holocausts. ¹The LORD called Moses, and from the meeting tent gave him this message: ²"Speak to the Israelites and tell them: When any one of you wishes to bring an animal offering to the LORD, such an offering must be

PART I: RITUAL OF SACRIFICES

Lev 1-7

It is helpful to begin reading the Book of Leviticus at Part IV, Code of Legal Holiness (chs. 17-26, pp. 54-81).

The first seven chapters of the book speak of ritual regulations for offering sacrifices and seem to take for granted that the reader has already been introduced to basic ideas of Israelite holiness. Chapters 1, 2, and 3 deal with burnt offerings (holocausts); chapters 4 and 5 generally speak of atonement sacrifices, while chapters 6 and 7 give special regulations for the priests.

Now that the presence of God finds a place in the midst of the people, in the tabernacle constructed by Moses (Exod 26-40), Moses is called by God to tell the people how to recognize the presence of the holy. If we read the first three chapters together, we can see that the same order runs throughout and that the emphasis is on obedience, which is the beginning of holiness.

1:1 Moses is still the mediator. Verses 1 and 2 are connecting links to the second and fourth books of Moses (Exodus and Numbers). Throughout Exodus, Yahweh tells Moses, "Speak to the Israelites." This phrase follows through Leviticus and on into Numbers. It acts as an introductory phrase to various regulations of worship and as an assertion of Israelite solidarity. A dispersed people needs to rally around their one leader and mediator Moses to celebrate their unity and solidarity.

The Hebrew title of this book, translated "and he called," is the first word of chapter 1. The "and" keeps us in contact with the call of Moses to build the Dwelling (Exod 24:16). Now that the Dwelling is complete, Moses is to act as the mediator of the worship action (Exod 40:32 and Lev 1:2). God calls Moses to speak the rules of worship for the people to obey. Moses is

from the herd or from the flock.
³"If his holocaust offering is from the herd, it must be a male without blemish. To find favor with the LORD, he shall bring it to the entrance of the meeting tent ⁴and there lay his hand on the head of the holocaust, so that it may be acceptable to make atonement for him. ⁵He shall then slaughter the bull before the LORD, but Aaron's sons, the priests, shall offer up its blood by splashing it on the sides of the altar which is at the entrance of the meeting tent. ⁶Then he shall skin the holocaust and cut it up into pieces. ⁷After Aaron's sons, the priests, have put some burning embers on the altar and laid some wood on them, ⁸they shall lay the pieces of meat, together with the head and the suet, on top of the wood and embers on the altar. ⁹The in-

the one mediator, and we are reminded again and again of the Torah instruction for the unity of the people under Moses.

1:3-9 To give oneself entirely to God. At first glance it seems that we are presented with just a number of ritual regulations. Our first impulse is to set them aside, turning away from the blood of the killing, the cutting-up and burning of animals. The stench of slaughter, squealing animals, and the choking smoke of carcasses in holocaust are repulsive to our Western atmosphere of liturgical banquet. We must consider, however, that this is the record of the people of God, a people who at this time in their history carried the painful memory of slavery in their very bones. And in view of the first law of the Sinai Covenant they needed to be weaned from the other gods to the one God Yahweh.

The incident of the worship of the molten calf along with the call to holiness on the part of the mediator Moses could have evoked some of the ritual response of the first chapters of Leviticus. Rituals attending animal sacrifice were not something new for their world. Their attempt, then, would be to return everything to Yahweh. The first command for the people is to divest the community of any alien allegiance and invest in the life of the one, holy God. The natural response would be to use the ritual practices already developed until a covenant relationship would dictate otherwise.

Disciplinary action because of infidelity seems also to have played a part in some of the ritual behavior. Whatever the history or initial reasons for some of the practices that seem so strange to us, the main purpose for including this material is to teach a lesson in obedience. The lesser member of a covenant relationship needs to learn this lesson first and witness to its exercise within the community in order to preserve the tradition. The accent is on an enduring obedience, since ritual expression can change its mode of expression. Without obedience there can be no life of holiness for the people.

One meaning of holiness is "wholeness." To be free from slavery and return to the Lord is to restore wholeness to life. Every corner of life needs to be continually examined and affirmed in the light of the call to wholeness.

ner organs and the shanks, however, the offerer shall first wash with water. The priest shall then burn the whole offering on the altar as a holocaust, a sweet-smelling oblation to the LORD.

¹⁰"If his holocaust offering is from the flock, that is, a sheep or a goat, he must bring a male without blemish. ¹¹This he shall slaughter before the LORD at the north side of the altar. Then Aaron's sons, the priests, shall splash its blood on the sides of the altar. ¹²When the offerer has cut it up into pieces, the priest shall lay these, together with the head

and suet, on top of the wood and the fire on the altar. ¹³The inner organs and the shanks, however, the offerer shall first wash with water. The priest shall offer them up and then burn the whole offering on the altar as a holocaust, a sweet-smelling oblation to the LORD.

¹⁴"If he offers a bird as a holocaust to the LORD, he shall choose a turtledove or a pigeon as his offering. ¹⁵Having brought it to the altar where it is to be burned, the priest shall snap its head loose and squeeze out its blood against the side of the altar. ¹⁶Its crop and

When this vocation is set to writing in the Hebrew way of thinking, it is no wonder that the song of Israel reaches our ears in a very concrete way, in what we might call fleshy terms (Exod 3:9; Lev 23; Deut 12:7). Just as it was the blood of Abel that cried out to God from the soil, so now the heart and flesh of this people cry out for the living God (Ps 84:3). Even the inner organs of the sacrificial animal are arranged in a special way and brought back in offering to the Lord of creation (Lev 1:8, 9, 13).

1:10-17 The sacrifice that goes up to the Lord. The three sacrifices of the bull (v. 5), the sheep or goat (v. 10), and the bird (v. 14) are described as holocausts (burnt offerings). The Hebrew verb simply means "to go up"; so the primary meaning of these offerings is to affirm the Lord as giver of the gift of life. The sacrifice is burnt up to the Lord. The smoke of the burning, along with the smoke of the sacred incense "going up" and covering up the smell of the slaughter, presents a sweet-smelling oblation to the Lord (Exod 30; Lev 1-8).

1:9, 13, 17 A sweet-smelling oblation. In Gen 8:21 the Lord smelled the sweet odor of Noah's offering and promised never again to doom the earth. In the Pentateuch God is spoken of in human terms and for God to smell the sweet-smelling odor is like saying that God is pleased with the sacrifice. This idea of the "sweet odor" is often repeated in the Pentateuch: in Exod 29 the ram, the unleavened food, and the lamb become sweet-smelling oblations (see also Lev 1-8, 23, 26 and Num 15, 18, 28, 29). Also in the flood story of Mesopotamia "the gods are smelling the savor of the sacrifices." This show of approval was probably used in Canaanite cult and taken over by the Israelites from the time when it was believed that the gods received nourishment from the smelling or inhaling of the burning food. Even the accounts of cereal and peace offerings conclude in this same way, "a sweet-smelling oblation to the Lord" (Lev 2 and 3).

feathers shall be removed and thrown on the ash heap at the east side of the altar. ¹⁷Then, having split the bird down the middle without separating the halves, the priest shall burn it on the altar, over the wood on the fire, as a holocaust, a sweet-smelling oblation to the LORD.

2 Cereal Offerings. ¹"When anyone wishes to bring a cereal offering to the LORD, his offering must consist of fine flour. He shall pour oil on it and put frankincense over it. ²When he has brought it to Aaron's sons, the priests, one of them shall take a handful of this

When the offering was wholly burned by the priest, a certain completeness, a holiness of the return of creation to the Lord, was expressed and experienced. It meant the same going-up or giving-up of self to God as a sweet-smelling oblation (1:4). Now the people had found a way to be wholly involved.

Note that usually the offerer performed the slaughter. The sprinkling, spilling, or splashing of the blood on the altar was reserved to the priests. The people brought the sacrificial victim to the entrance of the meeting tent where the whole community was included in the sacrifice action. There they were to accommodate and make holy the customs of the Canaanite people with whom they lived.

The Law given on Mount Sinai demanded complete obedience over the use of herd, flock, and grain (1–3). All creatures are included in "when any one of you." Even the poor, who otherwise might not be able to take part, can take from the turtledoves or pigeons plentiful in the area. Thus, Exod 19:6, "You shall be to me a kingdom of priests, a holy nation," could become a reality. By faithfully obeying these decrees, they would identify with the offerings and find favor as sweet-smelling oblations to the Lord.

Throughout Exodus, Leviticus, and Numbers, the Dwelling of the Lord is in the meeting tent. It is the place from which the call comes and it is the place of the sacrifice. In the offering the people and the priests are made holy by coming in contact with the presence of the Lord. The real and concrete thinking of the Hebrew mind speaks of the Lord calling from the meeting tent and of the people coming to the entrance of the tent in obedience (Lev 1:1-4). This action prepares for contact with holiness, and the sacrifice is not complete (holy) unless this condition is fulfilled (1:3; 3:8; 4:4).

2:11 Leaven or honey not to be burned. The offerings to be burned were already dead, but the action of yeast and the fermentation of the fruit syrup (included in the term honey) suggest something is still alive and, as such, could not be burned on the altar (2:11). In the Passover tradition (23) leaven was forbidden (Exod 12:15) and the people were to eat unleavened bread (*matzah*) for seven days (some say, in memory of the first seven days of the Exodus). One should also note that to carry unleavened bread is certainly a practical and secure way to keep wheat, barley, and oats when on a journey.

fine flour and oil, together with all the frankincense, and this he shall burn on the altar as a token offering, a sweet-smelling oblation to the Lord. ³The rest of the cereal offering belongs to Aaron and his sons. It is a most sacred oblation to the Lord.

⁴"When the cereal offering you present is baked in an oven, it must be in the form of unleavened cakes made of fine flour mixed with oil, or of unleavened wafers spread with oil. ⁵If you present a cereal offering that is fried on a griddle, it must be of fine flour mixed with oil and unleavened. ⁶Such a cereal offering must be broken into pieces, and oil must be poured over it. ⁷If you present a cereal offering that is prepared in a pot, it must be of fine flour, deep-fried in oil. ⁸A cereal offering that is made in any of these ways you shall bring to the Lord, offering it to the priest, who shall take it to the altar. ⁹Its token offering the priest shall then lift from the cereal offering and burn on the altar as a sweet-smelling oblation to the Lord. ¹⁰The rest of the

It is also stated that they had to leave Egypt in a hurry and had no time for the leavening action (Exod 12:33, 34). To eat unleavened bread would be a reminder of the hurried departure. This custom was kept in the feast of Unleavened Bread (Exod 12:17).

This latter feast was joined with the Passover feast, wherein a lamb was sacrificed and the blood was put on the doorposts as a sign for the Lord to pass over these houses. People on the move need to take along something to eat. Thus, both feasts came together quite naturally. Today, however, just the bread celebration remains. The Passover victim for the Jew is remembered only in the shankbone of the lamb and the order (*seder*) of the celebration. Both memorials are fused into one, called the Passover Seder (Lev 23). Within the Code of Holiness of the Book of Leviticus, these pilgrim feasts have their own particular emphasis.

We have cautioned not to read into the text more than can be seen at present. We should not, however, overlook a call to holiness that is conveyed by the sacred writer. To err in either regard would do an injustice to the living Word of God. So, in the Hebrew way of thinking, everything had to be brought to the Lord. Every slaughter, even killing for food, needed to be holy. It had to be in some way interpreted as a sacrifice, a making holy, since the blood shed had to return to the source of its life, the Creator. Life is in the blood (17:14; 19:26). For the people of God and those with whom they lived or who lived with them, every mark of living had to fall into the circle of the Holy (Exod 23).

This people struggled to respond to their call to holiness (wholeness). Such a struggle is the drive and desire of life itself to which the desire to survive is related. The duty now was to cooperate in a covenant with the Holy One present in their midst (Exod 19) and to bring about a certain completeness to their life and language (Exod 23). A covenant arrangement necessarily includes the condition of obedience for the one party and a recounting for the

cereal offering belongs to Aaron and his sons. It is a most sacred oblation to the LORD.

¹¹"Every cereal offering that you present to the LORD shall be unleavened, for you shall not burn any leaven or honey as an oblation to the LORD. ¹²Such you may indeed present to the LORD in the offering of first fruits, but they are not to be placed on the altar for a pleasing odor. ¹³However, every cereal offering that you present to the LORD shall be seasoned with salt. Do not let the salt of the covenant of your God be lacking from your cereal offering. On every offering you shall offer salt.

¹⁴"If you present a cereal offering of first fruits to the LORD, you shall offer it in the form of fresh grits of new ears of grain, roasted by fire. ¹⁵On this cereal offering you shall put oil and frankincense. ¹⁶For its token offering the priest shall then burn some of the grits and oil, together with all the frankincense, as an oblation to the LORD.

3 Peace Offerings. ¹"If someone in presenting a peace offering makes his offering from the herd, he may offer before the LORD either a male or a female animal, but it must be without blemish. ²He shall lay his hand on the head of his offering, and then slaughter it at the entrance of the meeting tent; but Aaron's sons, the priests, shall splash its blood on the sides of the altar. ³From the peace offering he shall offer as an oblation to the LORD the fatty membrane over the inner organs, and all the fat that adheres to them, ⁴as well as the two kidneys, with the fat on them near the loins, and the lobe of the liver, which he shall sever above the kidneys. ⁵All this Aaron's sons shall then burn on the altar with the holocaust, on the wood over the fire, as a sweet-smelling oblation to the LORD.

⁶"If the peace offering he presents to the LORD is from the flock, he may offer either a male or a female animal, but it must be without blemish. ⁷If he presents a lamb as his offering, he shall bring it

other of the blessings and curses that will follow upon obedience or disobedience to the covenant (Lev 26).

2:13 The salt of the covenant. Salt was a symbol of the lasting covenant, since salt kept food from spoiling. In ancient times partaking of salt together was a sign of friendship and alliance. There may also be a Hebrew wordplay on the word for salt which is related to the word for king. It is to God and God alone that the first obedience belongs, and this is the meaning of covenant obedience.

3:3, 16 "All the fat belongs to the Lord." References to food for the Lord may be for the Israelites honest attempts to gather in the practices of their neighbors and to return everything, including health, property, and the general well-being of the whole community, to the one, holy Lord.

There is a sharing of food (2:10; 3:9-11; 14-16), and thus, the custom of eating with the gods is now included (accommodated, sanctified) in the expression of the relation between the one God and the people, brought on by the covenant obedience. Even today we cement relationships by inviting one to share in a meal. Here is an outward expression in the act of obedience. In Hebrew belief and practice the presence of a neighbor affirmed the presence of God in their midst.

before the Lord, ⁸and after laying his hand on the head of his offering, he shall slaughter it before the meeting tent; but Aaron's sons shall splash its blood on the sides of the altar. ⁹As an oblation to the Lord he shall present the fat of the peace offering: the whole fatty tail, which he must sever close to the spine, the fatty membrane over the inner organs, and all the fat that adheres to them, ¹⁰as well as the two kidneys, with the fat on them near the loins, and the lobe of the liver, which he must sever above the kidneys. ¹¹All this the priest shall burn on the altar as the food of the Lord's oblation.

¹²"If he presents a goat, he shall bring it before the Lord, ¹³and after laying his hand on its head, he shall slaughter it before the meeting tent; but Aaron's sons shall splash its blood on the sides of the altar. ¹⁴From it he shall offer as an oblation to the Lord the fatty membrane over the inner organs, and all the fat that adheres to them, ¹⁵as well as the two kidneys, with the fat on them near the loins, and the lobe of the liver, which he must sever above the kidneys. ¹⁶All this the priest shall burn on the altar as the food of the sweet-smelling oblation. All the fat belongs to the Lord. ¹⁷This shall be a perpetual ordinance for your descendants wherever they may dwell. You shall not partake of any fat or any blood."

Burning the fat on the altar may have played a role in determining that the fatty portion belongs to the Lord. On hot fire grease will flare up and produce a cloud of smoke, perhaps reminiscent of the column of fire during the night and the column of cloud during the day (Exod 13). The Hebrews may have taken this graphic reminder as divine indication that this part of the victim belonged to the Lord.

Thus the fatty portion on the altar would cause great excitement. In the cloud (Exod 13:21; 16:10; 19:9; 24:16; 40:34; Lev 16:2, 13; Num 12:5) and in the column of fire (Exod 13:21, 22; 40:38), the Lord revealed the divine presence. God came to speak to Moses and through him to the people. (See Matt 17:5; Acts 1:9; 2 Pet 1:17; Rev 14:14—in these New Testament references and in the Old Testament references cited above, both the Hebrew and the Greek words for cloud and splendor are wrapped up in the idea of appearance-revelation.)

A concluding comment to chapters 1, 2, 3. The orderly arrangement of the material in these first three chapters may have also served as a memory aid, the key words being holocaust, cereal, and peace. The order has a certain holiness (completeness) in presenting the account of the sacrifices.

Chapters 4 and 5 exhibit an order that revolves not so much around the object of the sacrifice as around the disposition of the offerer. Sin and guilt are the subject matter, along with atonement for sin committed out of ignorance (4:1-35), out of omission (5:1-13), or by commission (5:14-26). These situations seem to cover the possible dispositions of the sinner and the offerings needed to atone for the situations (to make a person 'at-one' with God again) in the covenant relationship.

4 Sin Offerings: For Priests.

[1]The LORD said to Moses, [2]"Tell the Israelites: When a person inadvertently commits a sin against some command of the LORD by doing one of the forbidden things, [3]if it is the anointed priest who thus sins and thereby makes the people also become guilty, he shall present to the LORD a young, unblemished bull as a sin offering for the sin he committed. [4]Bringing the bullock to the entrance of the meeting tent, before the LORD, he shall lay his hand on its head and slaughter it before the LORD. [5]The anointed priest shall then take some of the bullock's blood and bring it into the meeting tent, [6]where, dipping his finger in the blood, he shall sprinkle it seven times before the LORD, toward the veil of the sanctuary. [7]The priest shall also put some of the blood on the horns of the altar of fragrant incense which is before the LORD in the meeting tent. The rest of the bullock's blood he shall pour out at the base of the altar of holocausts which is at the entrance of the meeting tent. [8]From the sin-offering bullock he shall remove all the fat: the fatty membrane over the inner organs, and all the fat that adheres to them, [9]as well as the two kidneys, with the fat on them near the loins, and the lobe of the liver, which he must sever above the kidneys. [10]This is the same as is removed from the ox of the peace offering; and the priest shall burn it on the altar of holocausts. [11]The hide of the bullock and all its flesh, with its head, legs, inner organs and offal, [12]in short, the whole bullock, shall be brought outside the camp to a clean place where the ashes are deposited and there be burned up in a wood fire. At the place of the ash heap, there it must be burned.

For the Community.

[13]"If the whole community of Israel inadvertently and without even being aware of it does something that the LORD has forbidden and thus makes itself guilty, [14]should it later on become known that the sin was committed, the community shall present a young bull as a sin offering. They shall bring it before the meeting tent, [15]and here, before the LORD, the elders of the community shall lay their hands on the bullock's head. When the bullock has been slaughtered before the LORD, [16]the anointed priest shall bring some of its blood into the meeting tent, [17]and dipping his finger in the blood, he shall sprinkle it seven times before the LORD, toward the veil. [18]He shall also put some of the blood on the horns of the altar of fragrant incense which is before the LORD in the meeting tent. The rest of the blood he shall pour out at the base of the altar of holocausts which is at the entrance of the meeting tent. [19]All of its fat

Chapters 4 and 5, sin and guilt offerings. In chapters 1, 2, and 3, sacrifices were brought out of obedience (because of the covenant), but willingly. In chapters 4 and 5 offerings of obligation are treated for those who are guilty of either unintentional (4:1-31) or intentional (5:1, 21-26) sins. In this covenant relation, since every action is in a relationship with God, every action is also related with everyone else involved in the same covenant. God is the source of life and the covenant is in a sense the return to life (Gen 2:7 and 6:17, 18). (The material is also summarized in Num 15:22-31.) The first person considered here is the priest who sins. The people are thereby also made guilty (Lev 4:3). Just as the priest offers on behalf of and along with the people, so the community is affected by other actions of the priest's life.

he shall take from it and burn on the altar, ²⁰doing with this bullock just as he did with the other sin-offering bullock. Thus the priest shall make atonement for them, and they will be forgiven. ²¹This bullock must also be brought outside the camp and burned, just as has been prescribed for the other one. This is the sin offering for the community.

For the Princes. ²²"Should a prince commit a sin inadvertently by doing one of the things which are forbidden by some commandment of the LORD, his God, and thus become guilty, ²³if later on he learns of the sin he committed, he shall bring as his offering an unblemished male goat. ²⁴Having laid his hands on its head, he shall slaughter the goat as a sin offering before the LORD, in the place where the holocausts are slaughtered. ²⁵The priest shall then take some of the blood of the sin offering on his finger and put it on the horns of the altar of holocausts. The rest of the blood he shall pour out at the base of this altar. ²⁶All of the fat he shall burn on the altar like the fat of the peace offering. Thus the priest shall make atonement for the prince's sin, and it will be forgiven.

For Private Persons. ²⁷"If a private person commits a sin inadvertently by doing one of the things which are forbidden by the commandments of the LORD, and thus becomes guilty, ²⁸should he later on learn of the sin he committed, he shall bring an unblemished she-goat

4:2 Inadvertent sin. All cases of ritual uncleanness which are unavoidable (for example, burying the dead) are included here. Note in Lev 4:1-12 that in the purification rite for a priest, the whole victim is disposed of outside the camp. Not even the hide is kept, to be given to the priest, as was the usual case (7:8). Now even the sanctuary is unclean, since the one who would usually receive the impurity of the people is himself unclean. There are other cases of inadvertent sin that affect the whole community (see Num 15:26, 27).

4:5-7 The blood rite. The angel of death passed over the houses on whose doorposts the blood of the Passover lamb was smeared (Exod 12:23). Here and in Lev 14:7 the blood is sprinkled before the Lord seven times. Some of the blood is put on the horns of the altar (Exod 29:12; Lev 8:15; 9:9). The sprinkling is a reminder of the blood of the covenant and its renewal (Exod 24:8). The smearing on the horns would remind one of every blood smearing: on the tent post in the field camp, the doorposts in the city, and on the altar at the foot of Mount Sinai. The basic idea was to ward off death and be attached to the source of life. In this case the intention is to be freed from the slavery of uncleanness, which divides the membership of the covenant, and to be restored as a full member of the human-divine community. The life that is in the blood is now returned to the Lord by actual contact with the altar. By this returning of life to the source of life, the individual, and thus the community, regains purity and the freedom to live again.

The whole community is affected by the impurity, even though it was committed by an individual. The reference to inadvertence is the attempt to cover every possible situation.

as the offering for his sin. ²⁹Having laid his hand on the head of the sin offering, he shall slaughter it at the place of the holocausts. ³⁰The priest shall then take some of its blood on his finger and put it on the horns of the altar of holocausts. The rest of the blood he shall pour out at the base of the altar. ³¹All the fat shall be removed, just as the fat is removed from the peace offering, and the priest shall burn it on the altar for an odor pleasing to the Lord. Thus the priest shall make atonement for him, and he will be forgiven.

³²"If, however, for his sin offering he presents a lamb, he shall bring an unblemished female. ³³Having laid his hand on its head, he shall slaughter this sin offering in the place where the holocausts are slaughtered. ³⁴The priest shall then take some of the blood of the sin offering on his finger and put it on the horns of the altar of holocausts. The rest of the blood he shall pour out at the base of the altar. ³⁵All the fat shall be removed, just as the fat is removed from the peace-offering lamb, and the priest shall burn it on the altar with the other oblations of the Lord. Thus the priest shall make atonement for the man's sin, and it will be forgiven.

5 For Special Cases. ¹"If any person refuses to give the information which, as a witness of something he has seen or learned, he has been adjured to give, and thus commits a sin and has guilt to bear; ²or if someone, without being aware of it, touches any unclean thing, as the carcass of an unclean wild animal, or that of an unclean domestic animal, or that of an unclean swarming creature, and thus becomes unclean and guilty; ³or if someone, without being aware of it, touches some human uncleanness, whatever kind of uncleanness this may be, and then recognizes his guilt; ⁴or if someone, without being aware of it, rashly utters an oath to do good or evil, such as men are accustomed to utter rashly, and then recognizes that he is guilty of such an oath; ⁵then whoever is guilty in any of these cases shall confess the sin he has incurred; ⁶and as his sin offering for the sin he has committed he shall bring to the Lord a female animal from the flock, a ewe lamb or a she-goat. The priest shall then make atonement for his sin.

⁷"If, however, he cannot afford an animal of the flock, he shall bring to the Lord as the sin offering for his sin two turtledoves or two pigeons, one for a sin

4:6 The blood is sprinkled seven times. Here and elsewhere (4:17; 14:7, 16, 27; 16:19; Num 19:4) the blood is sprinkled seven times. The number seven in ancient times was a sign of wholeness and completeness (holiness). Seven admits of a grouping of one flanked by two groups of three. Note the design of the menorah lampstand: a single center stem with two groups of three stems flanking the center. The menorah is the symbol of the perfect (holy) life. Many other examples could be cited in the use of seven as a sacred number. A primary example is the holy work of creation. God created the world in six days and then blessed the seventh day and made it holy (Gen 2:3). In Exod 31:15, the seventh day is a day of complete rest, sacred to the Lord.

5:1-26 Special cases. Here we sense the editors' insistence to include every possible situation of guilt and punishment, in reference not only to those

offering and the other for a holocaust. [8]He shall bring them to the priest, who shall offer the one for the sin offering first. Snapping its head loose at the neck, yet without breaking it off completely, [9]he shall sprinkle some of the blood of the sin offering against the side of the altar. The rest of the blood shall be squeezed out against the base of the altar. Such is the offering for sin. [10]The other bird shall be offered as a holocaust in the usual way. Thus the priest shall make atonement for the sin the man committed, and it will be forgiven.

[11]"If he is unable to afford even two turtledoves or two pigeons, he shall present as a sin offering for his sin one tenth of an ephah of fine flour. He shall not put oil or frankincense on it, because it is a sin offering. [12]When he has brought it to the priest, the latter shall take a handful of this flour as a token offering, and this he shall burn as a sin offering on the altar with the other oblations of the LORD. [13]Thus the priest shall make atonement for the sin that the man committed in any of the above cases, and it will be forgiven. The rest of the flour, like the cereal offerings, shall belong to the priest."

Guilt Offerings. [14]The LORD said to Moses, [15]"If someone commits a sin by inadvertently cheating in the LORD's sacred dues, he shall bring to the LORD as his guilt offering an unblemished ram from the flock, valued at two silver shekels according to the standard of the sanctuary shekel. [16]He shall also restore what he has sinfully withheld from the sanctuary, adding to it a fifth of its value. This is to be given to the priest, who shall then make atonement for him with the guilt-offering ram, and he will be forgiven.

[17]"If someone, without being aware of it, commits such a sin by doing one of the things which are forbidden by some commandment of the LORD, that he incurs guilt for which he must answer, [18]he shall bring as a guilt offering to the priest an unblemished ram of the flock of the established value. The priest shall then make atonement for the fault which was unwittingly committed, and it will be forgiven. [19]Such is the offering for guilt; the penalty of the guilt must be paid to the LORD."

[20]The LORD said to Moses, [21]"If someone commits a sin of dishonesty against the LORD by denying his neighbor a deposit or a pledge for a stolen article, or by otherwise retaining his neighbor's goods unjustly, [22]or if, having found a lost article, he denies the fact and swears falsely about it with any of the sinful oaths that men make in such cases, [23]he shall therefore, since he has incurred guilt by his sin, restore the thing that was stolen or unjustly retained by him or the deposit left with him or the lost article he found [24]or whatever else he swore falsely about; on the day of his guilt offering he shall make full restitution of the thing itself, and in addition, give the owner one fifth of its value. [25]As his guilt offering he shall bring to the LORD an unblemished ram of the flock of the established value. When he has presented this as his guilt offering to the priest, [26]the latter shall make atonement for him before the LORD, and he will be forgiven whatever guilt he may have incurred."

asked to testify about a particular case but even to those who know anything at all about another's sin (impurity), but refuse to testify. These latter also have a community responsibility to speak up. Note that the Hebrew word for guilt contains not only the conscious aspect of guilt from acting contrary to law (Torah) or the omission of a particular regulation but even self-accusation and the acceptance of the penalty.

6 **The Daily Holocaust.** ¹The LORD said to Moses, ²"Give Aaron and his sons the following command: This is the ritual for holocausts. The holocaust is to remain on the hearth of the altar all night until the next morning, and the fire is to be kept burning on the altar. ³The priest, clothed in his linen robe and wearing linen drawers on his body, shall take away the ashes to which the fire has reduced the holocaust on the altar, and lay them at the side of the altar. ⁴Then, having taken off these garments and put on other garments, he shall carry the ashes to a clean place outside the camp. ⁵The fire on the altar is to be kept burning; it must not go out. Every morning the priest shall put firewood on it. On this he shall lay out the holocaust and burn the fat of the peace offerings. ⁶The fire is to be kept burning continuously on the altar; it must not go out.

Daily Cereal Offering. ⁷"This is the ritual of the cereal offering. One of Aaron's sons shall first present it before the LORD, in front of the altar. ⁸Then he shall take from it a handful of its fine flour and oil, together with all the frankincense that is on it, and this he shall burn on the altar as its token offering, a sweet-smelling oblation to the LORD. ⁹The rest of it Aaron and his sons may eat; but it must be eaten in the form of unleavened cakes and in a sacred place: in the court of the meeting tent they shall eat it. ¹⁰It shall not be baked with leaven. I have given it to them as their portion from the oblations of the LORD; it is most sacred, like the sin offering and the guilt offering. ¹¹All the male descendants of Aaron may partake of it as their rightful share in the oblations of the LORD perpetually throughout your generations. Whatever touches the oblations becomes sacred."

¹²The LORD said to Moses, ¹³"This is the offering that Aaron and his sons shall present to the LORD [on the day he is anointed]: one tenth of an ephah of fine flour for the established cereal offering, half in the morning and half in the evening. ¹⁴It shall be well kneaded and fried in oil on a griddle when you bring it in. Having broken the offering into pieces, you shall present it as a sweet-smelling oblation to the LORD. ¹⁵Aaron's descendant who succeeds him as the anointed priest shall do likewise. This is a perpetual ordinance: for the LORD the whole offering shall be burned. ¹⁶Every cereal offering of a priest shall be a whole burnt offering; it may not be eaten."

Sin Offerings. ¹⁷The LORD said to

6:1–7:38 Answers to questions. Chapters 6 and 7 provide regulations that seemed to have developed from questions that came up while carrying out the basic ritual described in the first five chapters. For example, Where should this be done? What is the priest to wear? How should ashes be disposed of? What if the animal were wild and/or killed by a wild animal? As these questions were answered, they formed other regulations which eventually found their way into the Book of Leviticus. Additional regulations do not seem in any way to disturb the simple order of the first chapters. Note, however, the order that is preserved here. Chapter 6 deals with the material of chapters 1, 2, and 3 while chapter 7 gives some additions to chapters 4 and 5. But we must stress that everyone and everything must be included in the covenant. Nothing can be omitted in the gathering-in of even the slightest ritual regulations; every possible life-situation must be ordered as construction material for purity and the eventual life of holiness.

Moses, ¹⁸"Tell Aaron and his sons: This is the ritual for sin offerings. At the place where holocausts are slaughtered, there also, before the LORD, shall the sin offering be slaughtered. It is most sacred. ¹⁹The priest who presents the sin offering may partake of it; but it must be eaten in a sacred place, in the court of the meeting tent. ²⁰Whatever touches its flesh shall become sacred. If any of its blood is spilled on a garment, the stained part must be washed in a sacred place. ²¹A clay vessel in which it has been cooked shall thereafter be broken; if it is cooked in a bronze vessel, this shall be scoured afterward and rinsed with water. ²²All the males of the priestly line may partake of the sin offering, since it is most sacred. ²³But no one may partake of any sin offering of which some blood has been brought into the meeting tent to make atonement in the sanctuary; such an offering must be burned up in the fire.

7 Guilt Offerings. ¹"This is the ritual for guilt offerings, which are most sacred. ²At the place where the holocausts are slaughtered, there also shall the guilt offering be slaughtered. Its blood shall be splashed on the sides of the altar. ³All of its fat shall be taken from it and offered up: the fatty tail, the fatty membrane over the inner organs, ⁴as well as the two kidneys with the fat on them near the loins, and the lobe of the liver, which must be severed above the kidneys. ⁵All this the priest shall burn on the altar as an oblation to the LORD. This is the guilt offering. ⁶All the males of the priestly line may partake of it; but it must be eaten in a sacred place, since it is most sacred.

⁷"Because the sin offering and the guilt offering are alike, both having the same ritual, the guilt offering likewise belongs to the priest who makes atonement with it. ⁸Similarly, the priest who offers a holocaust for someone may keep for himself the hide of the holocaust that he has offered. ⁹Also, every cereal offering that is baked in an oven or deep-fried in a pot or fried on a griddle shall belong to the priest who offers it, ¹⁰whereas all cereal offerings that are offered up dry or mixed with oil shall belong to all of Aaron's sons without distinction.

Peace Offerings. ¹¹"This is the ritual for the peace offerings that are presented to the LORD. ¹²When anyone makes a peace offering in thanksgiving, together with his thanksgiving sacrifice he shall offer unleavened cakes mixed with oil, unleavened wafers spread with oil, and cakes made of fine flour mixed with oil and well kneaded. ¹³His offering shall

In chapter 7 we first meet the punishment of being "cut off from the people" (7:20, 21, 25, 27; 17:4, 9, 10, 14; 18:29; 19:8; 20:3, 5, 17, 18 and on into the Book of Numbers). Lev 17:10 and 20:6 make it clear that God, rather than the priest or people, will measure out this punishment. Some commentators interpret this penalty to be a premature death. It seems that this penalty is simply a statement of fact of what happens when one party violates the covenant. The Hebrew phrase for making a covenant is "to cut a covenant." So, in the violation of a covenant, one cuts oneself off from the other. Besides the Hebrew word-play, there is a good scare tactic in stating a fact. In eating the blood (17:10) and the wanton ways of the mediums (some may have been involved in neighboring blood rites, see 20:6), it would follow that this punishment would come from God, since the life is in the blood and God is the source of life. God would then be the immediate source of the punishment for the direct violation of life.

also include loaves of leavened bread along with the victim of his peace offering for thanksgiving. ¹⁴From each of his offerings he shall present one portion as a contribution to the LORD; this shall belong to the priest who splashes the blood of the peace offering.

¹⁵"The flesh of the thanksgiving sacrifice shall be eaten on the day it is offered; none of it may be kept till the next day. ¹⁶However, if the sacrifice is a votive or a free-will offering, it should indeed be eaten on the day the sacrifice is offered, but what is left over may be eaten on the next day. ¹⁷Should any flesh from the sacrifice be left over on the third day, it must be burned up in the fire. ¹⁸If, therefore, any of the flesh of the peace offering is eaten on the third day, it shall not win favor for him nor shall it be reckoned to his credit; rather, it shall be considered as refuse, and anyone who eats of it shall have his guilt to bear. ¹⁹Should the flesh touch anything unclean, it may not be eaten, but shall be burned up in the fire.

"All who are clean may partake of this flesh. ²⁰If, however, someone while in a state of uncleanness eats any of the flesh of a peace offering belonging to the LORD, that person shall be cut off from his people. ²¹Likewise, if someone touches anything unclean, whether the uncleanness be of human or of animal origin or from some loathsome crawling creature, and then eats of a peace offering belonging to the LORD, that person, too, shall be cut off from his people."

Prohibition against Blood and Fat. ²²The LORD said to Moses, ²³"Tell the Israelites: You shall not eat the fat of any ox or sheep or goat. ²⁴Although the fat of an animal that has died a natural death or has been killed by wild beasts may be put to any other use, you may not eat it. ²⁵If anyone eats the fat of an animal from which an oblation is made to the LORD, such a one shall be cut off from his people. ²⁶Wherever you dwell, you shall not partake of any blood, be it of bird or of animal. ²⁷Every person who partakes of any blood shall be cut off from his people."

The Portions for Priests. ²⁸The LORD said to Moses, ²⁹"Tell the Israelites: He who presents a peace offering to the

To avoid being cut off, in whatever way it could happen, is of special concern, for being excommunicated would not reflect the presence of the Holy One in the midst of the people. Later in chapter 20, we see the necessity of preserving the unity of the family and a proper order to the whole of one's life in order to preserve the community as a unit. In the community, the oneness of God is reflected. Therefore, one must avoid ever being cut off. In fact, everything concerning one's own life (and thus the community's life) must in some way move in relation to the Holy One. Belief is practice.

The order of belief and practice is obedience (chs. 1–27), then purification through ritual (chs. 11–27) and finally, sanctification (chs. 17–27). It seems as simple as the example of one who takes a prescription, finds healing, and then enjoys good health. The secret is in the "order" of making holy. And one experience does not end where the other begins. Obedience is at work in purity, both obedience and purity are at work in sanctification, and all three are fully alive in the life of holiness. However, if we concentrate on just one or try to escape from one into another, we find our life to be only an endless request of obedience. This could explain why the Book of Leviticus is often neglected or even avoided (see also Introduction, section 5).

LORD shall bring a part of it as his special offering to him, 30carrying in with his own hands the oblations to the LORD. The fat is to be brought in, together with the breast, which is to be waved as a wave offering before the LORD. 31The priest shall burn the fat on the altar, but the breast belongs to Aaron and his sons. 32Moreover, from your peace offering you shall give to the priest the right leg as a raised offering. 33The descendant of Aaron who offers up the blood and fat of the peace offering shall have the right leg as his portion, 34for from the peace offerings of the Israelites I have taken the breast that is waved and the leg that is raised up, and I have given them to Aaron, the priest, and to his sons by a perpetual ordinance as a contribution from the Israelites."

35This is the priestly share from the oblations of the LORD, allotted to Aaron and his sons on the day he called them to be the priests of the LORD; 36on the day he anointed them the LORD ordered the Israelites to give them this share by a perpetual ordinance throughout their generations.

37This is the ritual for holocausts, cereal offerings, sin offerings, guilt offerings, [ordination offerings] and peace offerings, 38which the LORD enjoined on Moses at Mount Sinai at the time when he commanded the Israelites in the wilderness of Sinai to bring their offerings to the LORD.

The overall arrangement in the book is very simple, but it is possible for the reader to become entangled in the many regulations and traditions. We need only witness the volumes upon volumes of legal transactions in our own court system with their varying decisions and changing regulations. Add to this the ease that oral traditions have of growing and changing of themselves. Then, even a long period of time may elapse before the oral traditions are written down. Finally we need to consider the time lapse of gathering the materials and the countless things that can happen between the gathering and the final editing. In the Book of Leviticus, the final editing seems to point to the very simple progression for living the life of holiness— obedience, purity, holiness.

PART II: CEREMONY OF ORDINATION

Lev 8–10

Chapters 8, 9, and 10 are a fitting place to introduce the dedication of the tabernacle and the ordination of the priest into the arrangement of the material for the Book of Leviticus. P, the Priestly writing, will continue later with the regulations for purity (chs. 11–16) and regulations for holiness (chs 17–27). Even though the ordination ceremony and the dedication of the tabernacle have already been explained in Exod 29, they are introduced again to keep the proper order of the holiness theme.

At the same time, we can almost hear the rhythmic beat and repetition of the life flow of the people: the arrival at and covenant on Sinai (Exod

II: CEREMONY OF ORDINATION

8 **Ordination of Aaron and His Sons.**
¹The LORD said to Moses, ²"Take
Aaron and his sons, together with the
vestments, the anointing oil, the bullock
for a sin offering, the two rams, and the
basket of unleavened food. ³Then
assemble the whole community at the
entrance of the meeting tent." ⁴And
Moses did as the LORD had commanded.
When the community had assembled at
the entrance of the meeting tent, ⁵Moses
told them what the LORD had ordered to
be done. ⁶Bringing forward Aaron and
his sons, he first washed them with
water. ⁷Then he put the tunic on Aaron,
girded him with the sash, clothed him
with the robe, placed the ephod on him,
and girded him with the embroidered
belt of the ephod, fastening it around
him. ⁸He then set the breastpiece on him,
with the Urim and Thummim in it, ⁹and
put the miter on his head, attaching the
gold plate, the sacred diadem, over the
front of the miter, at his forehead, as the
LORD had commanded him to do.
¹⁰Taking the anointing oil, Moses

anointed and consecrated the Dwelling,
with all that was in it. ¹¹Then he sprinkled some of this oil seven times on the
altar, and anointed the altar, with all its
appurtenances, and the laver, with its
base, thus consecrating them. ¹²He also
poured some of the anointing oil on
Aaron's head, thus consecrating him.
¹³Moses likewise brought forward
Aaron's sons, clothed them with tunics,
girded them with sashes, and put tur-
bans on them, as the LORD had commanded him to do.

Ordination Sacrifices. ¹⁴When he had
brought forward the bullock for a sin offering, Aaron and his sons laid their
hands on its head. ¹⁵Then Moses slaughtered it, and taking some of its blood,
with his finger he put it on the horns
around the altar, thus purifying the
altar. He also made atonement for the
altar by pouring out the blood at its base
when he consecrated it. ¹⁶Taking all the
fat that was over the inner organs, as
well as the lobe of the liver and the two
kidneys with their fat, Moses burned
them on the altar. ¹⁷The bullock,
however, with its hide and flesh and of-

19-24); the revelation of God (Exod 19); the tabernacle construction and
ceremony (Exod 25-28); the consecration of priests and altar (Exod 29); the
sabbath law (Exod 31); the sin (Exod 32); Moses the mediator (Exod 33);
the renewal of the covenant (Exod 34) and the giving of the sabbath law,
with regulations for the construction of the tabernacle (Exod 35-40); the
ceremony (Lev 1-7); the ordination of priests (Lev 8-10); the cleansing of
the sanctuary, priests, and people (Lev 11-16); a new covenant life (Lev
17-27); and the revelation of God. This rhythmic beat is not just a mean-
ingless repetition. Each time the statement of life is given in the heartbeat
of the people.

Signs of life, maturing, and new insights are evident. The placing of
chapters 1-7 where they are points out the necessity of obedience to the ritual
of sacrifice. This ritual expresses both the desire for holiness and the condi-
tioning element for purification. All this is antecedent to the life and practice of holiness (chs. 17-26).

8:1-36 The ordination ceremony. Moses is the mediator even of the
priesthood (vv. 1-4). A more detailed description of the vestments and
ceremonies has already been given in Exod 28-29. In keeping with the theme

fal he burned in the fire outside the camp, as the Lᴏʀᴅ had commanded him to do.

¹⁸He next brought forward the holocaust ram, and Aaron and his sons laid their hands on its head. ¹⁹When he had slaughtered it, Moses splashed its blood on all sides of the altar. ²⁰After cutting up the ram into pieces, he burned the head, the cut-up pieces and the suet; ²¹then, having washed the inner organs and the shanks with water, he also burned these remaining parts of the ram on the altar as a holocaust, a sweet-smelling oblation to the Lᴏʀᴅ, as the Lᴏʀᴅ had commanded him to do.

²²Then he brought forward the second ram, the ordination ram, and Aaron and his sons laid their hands on its head. ²³When he had slaughtered it, Moses took some of its blood and put it on the tip of Aaron's right ear, on the thumb of his right hand, and on the big toe of his right foot. ²⁴Moses had the sons of Aaron also come forward, and he put some of the blood on the tips of their right ears, on the thumbs of their right hands, and on the big toes of their right feet. The rest of the blood he splashed on the sides of the altar. ²⁵He then took the fat: the fatty tail and all the fat over the inner organs, the lobe of the liver and the two kidneys with their fat, and likewise the right leg; ²⁶from the basket of unleavened food that was set before the Lᴏʀᴅ he took one unleavened cake, one loaf of bread made with oil, and one wafer; these he placed on top of the portions of fat and the right leg. ²⁷He then put all these things into the hands of Aaron and his sons, whom he had wave them as a wave offering before the Lᴏʀᴅ.

²⁸When he had received them back, Moses burned them with the holocaust on the altar as the ordination offering, a sweet-smelling oblation to the Lᴏʀᴅ. ²⁹He then took the breast and waved it as a wave offering before the Lᴏʀᴅ; this was Moses' own portion of the ordination ram. All this was in keeping with the Lᴏʀᴅ's command to Moses. ³⁰Taking some of the anointing oil and some of the blood that was on the altar, Moses sprinkled with it Aaron and his vestments, as well as his sons and their vestments, thus consecrating both Aaron and his vestments and his sons and their vestments.

³¹Finally, Moses said to Aaron and his sons, "Boil the flesh at the entrance of the meeting tent, and there eat it with the bread that is in the basket of the ordination offering, in keeping with the command I have received: 'Aaron and his sons shall eat of it.' ³²What is left over of the flesh and the bread you shall burn up in the fire. ³³Moreover, you are not to depart from the entrance of the meeting tent for seven days, until the days of your ordination are completed; for your ordination is to last for seven days. ³⁴The Lᴏʀᴅ has commanded that what has been done today be done to make atonement for you. ³⁵Hence you must remain at the entrance of the meeting tent day and night for seven days, carrying out the prescriptions of the Lᴏʀᴅ; otherwise you shall die; for this is the command I have received." ³⁶So Aaron and his sons did all that the Lᴏʀᴅ had commanded through Moses.

9 **Octave of the Ordination.** ¹On the eighth day Moses summoned Aaron and his sons, together with the elders of

of Leviticus, the *order* to be followed in the ordination ceremony (vv. 5-33) is affirmed. Stress is put upon atonement for the altar and for the ones being ordained (vv. 15, 34), identifying them with the victim of sacrifice (vv. 22-31), rather than stressing their appointment by God through Moses (v. 35).

9:1-7 The octave (eighth day) sacrifice. The sacrifice completes the consecration of the priest. It consists of a combination of a calf-sin offering, a

Israel, ²and said to Aaron, "Take a calf for a sin offering and a ram for a holocaust, both without blemish, and offer them before the LORD. ³Tell the elders of Israel, too: Take a he-goat for a sin offering, a calf and a lamb, both unblemished yearlings, for a holocaust, ⁴and an ox and a ram for a peace offering, to sacrifice them before the LORD, along with a cereal offering mixed with oil; for today the LORD will reveal himself to you." ⁵So they brought what Moses had ordered. When the whole community had come forward and stood before the LORD, ⁶Moses said, "This is what the LORD orders you to do, that the glory of the LORD may be revealed to you. ⁷Come up to the altar," Moses then told Aaron, "and offer your sin offering and your holocaust in atonement for yourself and for your family; then present the offering of the people in atonement for them, as the LORD has commanded."

⁸Going up to the altar, Aaron first slaughtered the calf that was his own sin offering. ⁹When his sons presented the blood to him, he dipped his finger in the blood and put it on the horns of the altar. The rest of the blood he poured out at the base of the altar. ¹⁰He then burned on the altar the fat, the kidneys and the lobe of the liver that were taken from the sin offering, as the LORD had commanded Moses; ¹¹but the flesh and the hide he burned up in the fire outside the camp. ¹²Then Aaron slaughtered his holocaust. When his sons brought him the blood, he splashed it on all sides of the altar. ¹³They then brought him the pieces and the head of the holocaust, and he burned them on the altar. ¹⁴Having washed the inner organs and the shanks, he burned these also with the holocaust on the altar.

¹⁵Thereupon he had the people's offering brought up. Taking the goat that was for the people's sin offering, he slaughtered it and offered it up for sin as before. ¹⁶Then he brought forward the holocaust, other than the morning holocaust, and offered it in the usual manner. ¹⁷He then presented the cereal offering; taking a handful of it, he burned it on the altar. ¹⁸Finally he slaughtered the ox and the ram, the peace offering of the people. When his sons brought him the blood, Aaron splashed it on all sides of the altar. ¹⁹The portions of fat from the ox and from the ram, the fatty tail, the fatty membrane over the inner organs, the two kidneys, with the fat that is on them, and the lobe of the liver, ²⁰he placed on top of the breasts and burned them on the altar, ²¹having first waved the breasts and the right legs as a wave offering before the LORD, in keeping with the LORD's command to Moses.

ram-holocaust (on the part of a high priest), and a he-goat sin offering. A calf and lamb for a holocaust, and an ox and ram for a peace offering, along with a cereal offering mixed with oil, are also offered on the eighth day. What a tremendous celebration that includes virtually all the sacrifices at which the priest later assists. The celebration is magnificent, for on that day, the "glory of the Lord was revealed to all the people" (v. 23; see also vv. 4, 6).

The writer or writers seem to convey two essential marks of the priesthood. First, as for the intercessory duty of the priest, every sacrifice needed to be brought forth to stand before the Lord. The priests were to intercede regarding decisions already made and ones for which understanding was needed. This is what making holy was all about—to be present to the presence of the Lord (9:5). The priest is to "keep in touch" with the Lord.

Revelation of the Lord's Glory. 22Aaron then raised his hands over the people and blessed them. When he came down from offering the sin offering and holocaust and peace offering, 23Moses and Aaron went into the meeting tent. On coming out they again blessed the people. Then the glory of the LORD was revealed to all the people. 24Fire came forth from the LORD's presence and consumed the holocaust and the remnants of the fat on the altar. Seeing this, all the people cried out and fell prostrate.

10 Nadab and Abihu. 1During this time Aaron's sons Nadab and Abihu took their censers and, strewing incense on the fire they had put in them, they offered up before the LORD profane fire, such as he had not authorized. 2Fire therefore came forth from the LORD's presence and consumed them, so that they died in his presence. 3Moses then said to Aaron, "This is as the LORD said:

Through those who approach me I will
    manifest my sacredness;
  In the sight of all the people I will
    reveal my glory."

But Aaron said nothing. 4Then Moses summoned Mishael and Elzaphan, the sons of Aaron's uncle Uzziel, with the order, "Come, remove your kinsmen from the sanctuary and carry them to a place outside the camp." 5So they went in and took them, in their tunics, outside the camp, as Moses had commanded.

Conduct of the Priests. 6Moses said to Aaron and his sons Eleazar and Ithamar, "Do not bare your heads or tear your garments, lest you bring not only death on yourselves but God's wrath also on the whole community. Your kinsmen, the rest of the house of Israel, shall mourn for those whom the LORD's fire has smitten; 7but do not you go beyond the entry of the meeting tent, else you shall die; for the anointing oil of the LORD is upon you." So they did as Moses told them.

8The LORD said to Aaron, 9"When you are to go to the meeting tent, you and your sons are forbidden under pain of death, by a perpetual ordinance throughout your generations, to drink any wine or strong drink. 10You must be able to distinguish between what is

The community had to present itself at the entrance of the tent and then come to the altar in the person of the priest (v. 7). The divine power could then be at work in the midst of the people, through the priest in touch with the presence of God. The second essential which the writers seem to be intent on was Moses as the mediator. He was the prophet to Pharaoh. He acted as the king in leading the people out of Egypt. He is now the high priest in the sacrifice and the ordination of those who will assist in sacrifice.

10:1-5 Death of Nadab and Abihu. Some have suggested that Aaron's sons Nadab and Abihu had filled their containers with fire that was not holy, that is, taken from a place other than the altar. Others say that their incense was not the clean mixture it should have been. Thus, they were punished with death by fire, a holy fire from the altar. Lightning could have struck them dead. Since they were at the altar at the time, the people would certainly interpret any happening as coming from the Lord.

10:9-10 Ability to distinguish. Whatever happened, the main point is brought out in verses 9 and 10, where Moses says that no wine or strong drink is to be taken before priestly duty at the meeting tent. "You must be

sacred and what is profane, between what is clean and what is unclean; ¹¹you must teach the Israelites all the laws that the LORD has given them through Moses."

The Eating of the Priestly Portions. ¹²Moses said to Aaron and his surviving sons, Eleazar and Ithamar, "Take the cereal offering left over from the oblations of the LORD, and eat it beside the altar in the form of unleavened cakes. Since it is most sacred, ¹³you must eat it in a sacred place. This is your due from the oblations of the LORD, and that of your sons; such is the command I have received. ¹⁴With your sons and daughters you shall also eat the breast of the wave offering and the leg of the raised offering, in a clean place; for these have been assigned to you and your children as your due from the peace offerings of the Israelites. ¹⁵The leg of the raised offering and the breast of the wave offering shall first be brought in with the oblations, the fatty portions, that are to be waved as a wave offering before the LORD. Then they shall belong to you and your children by a perpetual ordinance, as the LORD has commanded."

¹⁶When Moses inquired about the goat of the sin offering, he discovered that it had all been burned. So he was angry with the surviving sons of Aaron, Eleazar and Ithamar, and said, ¹⁷"Why did you not eat the sin offering in the sacred place, since it is most sacred? It has been given to you that you might bear the guilt of the community and make atonement for them before the LORD. ¹⁸If its blood was not brought into the inmost part of the sanctuary, you should certainly have eaten the offering in the sanctuary, in keeping with the command I had received." ¹⁹Aaron answered Moses, "Even though they pre-

able to distinguish between the sacred and profane." So, in the seven-day celebration, it could be that Aaron and his sons might have imbibed too much wine. Even though Nadab and Abihu could have been struck by lightning, it is possible that they put the wrong mixture on the fire, resulting in a flare up and consequent asphyxiation (since v. 5 says they were buried in their tunics).

In view of other references in Exod 24 and Num 3, and aside from the Moses injunction to avoid on-the-job drinking of wine or other strong drink (10:9), we would do well to look further. The moment is very sacred: "Through those who approach me I will manifest my sacredness; in the sight of all the people, I will reveal my glory (10:3)." Abihu ("He is my father") and Nadab ("Na is generous") might also represent an earlier priesthood now replaced by the Aaronic and Levitical priesthood. The incident, then, is used here to introduce, in a literary but nonetheless real way, the new order (or at least the demise of the old). It is now through Aaron and his sons that both the new and the old are represented at the ordination ceremony (10:3). Other sacrifices of fire are forbidden. Recall in chapter 9, after the seven-day ordination ceremony, that on the eighth day the people saw the glory of the Lord coming forth in the form of fire from the Lord's presence. If lightning occurred, it would have given occasion for an explanation.

10:11 The priests are to teach the Torah. There is an interesting and added responsibility for the priest in regard to preparation for and maturing

sented their sin offering and holocaust before the LORD today, yet this misfortune has befallen me. Had I then eaten of the sin offering today, would it have been pleasing to the LORD?" [20]On hearing this, Moses was satisfied.

in holiness. He is to be a teacher of the Torah, "all the laws that the Lord has given through Moses" (v. 11—once again, an insistence on Moses as the mediator). The Hebrew word means both "to teach," and "to direct." The priest is to learn the proper direction (order) and then teach others. In English we have the fuller meaning in basically the same word, which now has the meaning of "disciple" and "discipline."

PART III: LAWS REGARDING LEGAL PURITY

Lev 11–16

The insertion here of the chapters on the priesthood is natural. Otherwise, obedience might be practiced for obedience's sake. Obedience has now become a response to the covenant relation through the mediation of the priesthood and continues to be alive in the purification-preparation (chs. 11–16) for holiness (chs. 17–27).

Now legal purity (chs. 11–15) will be explained and emphasized as a condition, along with obedience, for legal holiness that comes later (chs. 17–27). (Chapter 16 is a bridge-chapter for chapters 11–15 and 17–27.)

Recalling what has been said about Hebrew thought patterns, we can respect these regulations as alive, not simply as directions for life. They all point to and are part of the life of holiness or completeness—to be fully alive is to respect the power of the Creator of life. It seems that the final editors laid a very simple pathway to holiness. They realized that now was the time, in the whole body of the Torah, to mention this Levitical regulation. Without it, the Torah would be without a heart and its beat. The beat should be an evident sign of the presence of the Holy and the expression of the fullness of life, the Code of Holiness in 17–26 (ch. 27 is another bridge-chapter). Since the Book of Leviticus is the heart of the Torah, we refer to the Code of Holiness as the beat of that heart.

For those who are to become holy, the Lord says, "Speak to the whole Israelite community and tell them, 'Be holy, for I, the Lord, your God, am holy'" (Lev 20:7; Exod 31:13; and Lev 11:44). Obedience comes first (chs. 1–7); then the Lord manifests his glory to the people through the holy priesthood-group of the community (chs. 8–10). But before one can experience holiness, one must be clean (pure) (chs. 11–16). And since "cleanliness is next

III: LAWS REGARDING LEGAL PURITY

11 **Clean and Unclean Food.** ¹The LORD said to Moses and Aaron, ²"Speak to the Israelites and tell them: Of all land animals these are the ones you may eat: ³any animal that has hoofs you may eat, provided it is cloven-footed and chews the cud. ⁴But you shall not eat any of the following that only chew the cud or only have hoofs: the camel, which indeed chews the cud, but

to Godliness," so purity which results from obedience to the law comes next to holiness. This is the material treated next on the way to holiness. Obedience, purity, and holiness cannot be separated any more than can body, blood, and soul. (In Hebrew thinking, these latter three are included in the one word "being.") It is important to consider this way of thinking if we are to understand the way the Levitical material conveys the meaning of holiness. Obedience is included in the understanding and experience of purity. The regulations now become more exacting. Purity conditions one for the Code of Holiness.

Since purity can come only from God, the presence of God must be in the midst of the people, above the ark (16:2). This is the place of atonement in which is contained the forgiveness and reconciliation which result in purity.

Chapters 11–16 tell how the condition of purity is established. The materials brought together in these regulations present a fit (pure) receptacle, 'for-giving' of holiness. This last sentence contains the ideas of forgiveness and the condition needed for holiness. It is one thing to be forgiven, but it is another to live a life of holiness. The state of purity resulting from the forgiveness of God is the receptacle for the life of holiness; it is not the state of holiness. This is why, once a year, even to this day, atonement is made for all the sins on the feast of Yom Kippur, the Day of Atonement.

This explains the placement of the Code of Holiness (chs. 17–27) in the Book of Leviticus; there is an orderly progression to the fullness of life, the life of holiness (19:1-7). It also explains the placement of the bridge-chapter 16 with the Day of Atonement, the ongoing condition for the life of holiness. Later we will see how chapter 27 also becomes a bridge-chapter, following the presentation of the material on holiness.

Chapters 11–16 concern the clean and the unclean. Chapters 11 and 12 consider what is taken internally: clean and unclean food and the uncleanness of childbirth resulting in loss of blood (the seed was taken internally). What shows up externally on the skin or garments is the subject of chapters 13 and 14. Chapter 15 deals with what flows from within a person. The well-known chapter 16, giving the account of the Day of Atonement, is the important bridge-chapter connecting the clean (pure) and the holy.

11:1-23 Clean and unclean food: the dietary laws. Animals that may and may not be eaten are listed here: those of the land (vv. 1-8), of the sea

does not have hoofs and is therefore unclean for you; ⁵the rock badger, which indeed chews the cud, but does not have hoofs and is therefore unclean for you; ⁶the hare, which indeed chews the cud, but does not have hoofs and is therefore unclean for you; and the pig, ⁷which does indeed have hoofs and is cloven-footed, but does not chew the cud and is therefore unclean for you. ⁸Their flesh you shall not eat, and their dead bodies you shall not touch; they are unclean for you.

⁹"Of the various creatures that live in the water, you may eat the following: whatever in the seas or in river waters has both fins and scales you may eat. ¹⁰But of the various creatures that crawl or swim in the water, whether in the sea or in the rivers, all those that lack either fins or scales are loathsome for you, ¹¹and you shall treat them as loathsome. Their flesh you shall not eat, and their dead bodies you shall loathe. ¹²Every water creature that lacks fins or scales is loathsome for you.

¹³"Of the birds, these you shall loathe and, as loathsome, they shall not be eaten: the eagle, the vulture, the osprey, ¹⁴the kite, the various species of falcons, ¹⁵the various species of crows, ¹⁶the ostrich, the nightjar, the gull, various species of hawks, ¹⁷the owl, the cormorant, the screech owl, ¹⁸the barn owl, the desert owl, the buzzard, ¹⁹the stork, the various species of herons, the hoopoe, and the bat.

²⁰"The various winged insects that

(vv. 9-12), and of the air (vv. 13-19), and finally, those found in all three areas—insects and swarming creatures (vv. 20-23).

The dead bodies of the unclean must not be touched or else one becomes unclean (vv. 24-32). For the most part these regulations are repeated in Deut 14:3-20. Both in Leviticus and Deuteronomy the people are warned to make themselves holy and to keep themselves holy by simply avoiding certain foods (Lev 11 and Deut 14:3-21). However, a straightforward reason why certain foods cause uncleanness or defilement is not known. Simple obedience seems to be a good reason in view of Gen 2:16 wherein God initially said, "You are free to eat . . . except . . ." Even today, there are certain foods permitted by Jewish dietary regulation, called *kosher*, which means "proper" to eat.

Sometimes assumptions are made concerning Israelite relationship with the cult practice of their neighbors. Even though some literary references have emerged, we need to be cautious and apply studied research for further evidence of real life associations. There seems to have been a common cult language used in the Near East. From this base every tribe or nation took what would best express their relationship with the presence of the Holy in the whole of creation (*see also* Introduction, 7. D).

The simple and clear thrust of this material in Leviticus seems to be that everyone and everything must be brought into the order and dominion of the one, holy God. The whole of creation had already been joined to God's order and dominion in the creation stories of Genesis; now the worship-life of the people is directed to that God. The Tabernacle had just been erected (Exod 40), and now the time had come for the "Levitical material" to go

walk on all fours are loathsome for you. 21But of the various winged insects that walk on all fours you may eat those that have jointed legs for leaping on the ground; 22hence of these you may eat the following: the various kinds of locusts, the various kinds of grasshoppers, the various kinds of katydids, and the various kinds of crickets. 23All other winged insects that have four legs are loathsome for you.

24"Such is the uncleanness that you contract, that everyone who touches their dead bodies shall be unclean until evening, 25and everyone who picks up any part of their dead bodies shall wash his garments and be unclean until evening. 26All hoofed animals that are not cloven-footed or do not chew the cud are unclean for you; everyone who touches them becomes unclean. 27Of the various quadrupeds, all those that walk on paws are unclean for you; everyone who touches their dead bodies shall be unclean until evening, 28and everyone who picks up their dead bodies shall wash his garments and be unclean until evening. Such is their uncleanness for you.

29"Of the creatures that swarm on the ground, the following are unclean for you: the rat, the mouse, the various kinds of lizards, 30the gecko, the chameleon, the agama, the skink, and the mole. 31Among the various swarming creatures, these are unclean for you. Everyone who touches them when they are dead shall be unclean until evening. 32Everything on which one of them falls when dead becomes unclean. Any such article that men use, whether it be an article of wood, cloth, leather or goat hair,

must be put in water and remain unclean until evening, when it again becomes clean. 33Should any of these creatures fall into a clay vessel, everything in it becomes unclean, and the vessel itself you must break. 34Any solid food that was in contact with water, and any liquid that men drink, in any such vessel become unclean. 35Any object on which one of their dead bodies falls, becomes unclean; if it is an oven or a jar-stand, this must be broken to pieces; they are unclean and shall be treated as unclean by you. 36However, a spring or a cistern for collecting water remains clean; but whoever touches the dead body becomes unclean. 37Any sort of cultivated grain remains clean even though one of their dead bodies falls on it; 38but if the grain has become moistened, it becomes unclean when one of these falls on it.

39"When one of the animals that you could otherwise eat, dies of itself, anyone who touches its dead body shall be unclean until evening; 40and anyone who eats of its dead body shall wash his garments and be unclean until evening; so also, anyone who removes its dead body shall wash his garments and be unclean until evening.

41"All the creatures that swarm on the ground are loathsome and shall not be eaten. 42Whether it crawls on its belly, goes on all fours, or has many legs, you shall eat no swarming creature: they are loathsome. 43Do not make yourselves loathsome or unclean with any swarming creature through being contaminated by them. 44For I, the LORD, am your God; and you shall make and keep your-

through the Holy Place in preparation for entry into the Holy of Holies. The experience of the divine-human relationship could be lived out even in the written record of this people. As St. Jerome remarked, "There is an odor of holiness about the book of Leviticus."

11:36 A spring or cistern remains pure. The purity of water was necessary, not only because drinking water was scarce but also because this

selves holy, because I am holy. You shall not make yourselves unclean, then, by any swarming creature that crawls on the ground. ⁴⁵Since I, the LORD, brought you up from the land of Egypt that I might be your God, you shall be holy, because I am holy.

⁴⁶"This is the law for animals and birds and for all the creatures that move about in the water or swarm on the ground, ⁴⁷that you may distinguish between the clean and the unclean, between creatures that may be eaten and those that may not be eaten."

12 **Uncleanness of Childbirth.** ¹The LORD said to Moses, ²"Tell the Israelites: When a woman has conceived and gives birth to a boy, she shall be unclean for seven days, with the same uncleanness as at her menstrual period. ³On the eighth day, the flesh of the boy's foreskin shall be circumcised, ⁴and then she shall spend thirty-three days more in becoming purified of her blood; she shall

not touch anything sacred nor enter the sanctuary till the days of her purification are fulfilled. ⁵If she gives birth to a girl, for fourteen days she shall be as unclean as at her menstruation, after which she shall spend sixty-six days in becoming purified of her blood.

⁶"When the days of her purification for a son or for a daughter are fulfilled, she shall bring to the priest at the entrance of the meeting tent a yearling lamb for a holocaust and a pigeon or a turtledove for a sin offering. ⁷The priest shall offer them up before the LORD to make atonement for her, and thus she will be clean again after her flow of blood. Such is the law for the woman who gives birth to a boy or a girl child. ⁸If, however, she cannot afford a lamb, she may take two turtledoves or two pigeons, the one for a holocaust and the other for a sin offering. The priest shall make atonement for her, and thus she will again be clean."

water had not yet been drawn out by human hands. The water is holy because its present source is the ground (spring) or heaven (rain in the cistern).

12:1-8 Uncleanness of childbirth. The reason for this defilement is found in verse 7: "Thus, she will be clean again after her flow of blood." It is the flow of blood that defiles. (The life is in the blood and because the flow is recurrent, proper control cannot be maintained. Lev 15:32-33 mentions that men and women are treated alike.) They could only come to the entrance of the tent or, in another time, they were barred from the temple mound.

Today there is still a great deal of mystery and pain connected with menstruation and childbirth. We have unraveled some of the mystery, but the pain remains (Gen 3:16). At that time fear and taboo also played a part in the experience. The afterbirth might tend to make one think that some kind of punishment was being put upon a person. And, of course, there were the stories and taboos of neighbors. The rate of miscarriage may also have been high. This would accentuate the need to explain the disorder and call for a regulation concerning defilement and the need for purification.

The offering is made only after the flow stops (Lev 15:13-14, 28-29), so there is no question of practicing magic—a ritual performed in order to bring about some change.

12:2, 5 The doubling of purification time for females. This may have

13 **Leprosy.** [1]The Lord said to Moses and Aaron, [2]"If someone has on his skin a scab or pustule or blotch which appears to be the sore of leprosy, he shall be brought to Aaron, the priest, or to one of the priests among his descendants, [3]who shall examine the sore on his skin. If the hair on the sore has turned white and the sore itself shows that it has penetrated below the skin, it is indeed the sore of leprosy; the priest, on seeing this, shall declare the man unclean. [4]If, however, the blotch on the skin is white, but does not seem to have penetrated below the skin, nor has the hair turned white, the priest shall quarantine the stricken man for seven days. [5]On the seventh day the priest shall again examine him. If he judges that the sore has remained unchanged and has not spread on the skin, the priest shall quarantine him for another seven days, [6]and once more examine him on the seventh day. If the sore is now dying out and has not spread on the skin, the priest shall declare the man clean; it was merely eczema. The man shall wash his garments and so become clean. [7]But if, after he has shown himself to the priest to be declared clean, the eczema spreads at all on his skin, he shall once more show himself to the priest. [8]Should the priest, on examining it, find that the eczema has indeed spread on the skin, he shall declare the man unclean; it is leprosy.

[9]"When someone is stricken with leprosy, he shall be brought to the priest. [10]Should the priest, on examining him, find that there is a white scab on the skin which has turned the hair white and that there is raw flesh in it, [11]it is skin leprosy that has long developed. The priest shall declare the man unclean without first quarantining him, since he is certainly unclean. [12]If leprosy breaks out on the skin and, as far as the priest can see, covers all the skin of the stricken man from head to foot, [13]should the priest then, on examining him, find that the leprosy does cover his whole body, he shall declare the stricken man clean; since it has all turned white, the man is clean. [14]But as soon as raw flesh appears on him, he is unclean; [15]on observing the raw flesh, the priest shall declare him unclean, because raw flesh is unclean; it is leprosy. [16]If, however, the raw flesh again turns white, he shall return to the priest; [17]should the latter, on examining him, find that the sore has indeed turned white, he shall declare the stricken man clean, and thus he will be clean.

[18]"If a man who had a boil on his skin which later healed, [19]should now in the place of the boil have a white scab or a pink blotch, he shall show himself to the priest. [20]If the latter, on examination, sees that it is deeper than the skin and that the hair has turned white, he shall declare the man unclean: it is the sore of leprosy that has broken out in the boil. [21]But if the priest, on examining him, finds that there is no white hair in it and that it is not deeper than the skin and is already dying out, the priest shall quarantine him for seven days. [22]If it has then spread on the skin, the priest shall declare him unclean; the man is stricken. [23]But if the blotch remains in its place without spreading, it is merely the scar

something to do with menstrual flow. Remember, the life is in the blood and every precaution must be taken to recognize God as the source of life.

13:4 Seven-day quarantine. This is probably a practical precaution in the case of skin disorder. Any change in the skin should take place by then so that the priest can decide about the purity of the person. The waiting is made holy by choosing seven days.

of the boil; the priest shall therefore declare him clean.

24"If a man had a burn on his skin, and the proud flesh of the burn now becomes a pink or a white blotch, 25the priest shall examine it. If the hair has turned white on the blotch and this seems to have penetrated below the skin, it is leprosy that has broken out in the burn; the priest shall therefore declare him unclean and stricken with leprosy. 26But if the priest, on examining it, finds that there is no white hair on the blotch and that this is not deeper than the skin and is already dying out, the priest shall quarantine him for seven days. 27Should the priest, when examining it on the seventh day, find that it has spread at all on the skin, he shall declare the man unclean and stricken with leprosy. 28But if the blotch remains in its place without spreading on the skin and is already dying out, it is merely the scab of the burn; the priest shall therefore declare the man clean, since it is only the scar of the burn.

29"When a man or a woman has a sore on the head or cheek, 30should the priest, on examining it, find that the sore has penetrated below the skin and that there is fine yellow hair on it, the priest shall declare the person unclean, for this is scall, a leprous disease of the head or cheek. 31But if the priest, on examining the scall sore, finds that it has not penetrated below the skin, though the hair on it may not be black, the priest shall quarantine the person with scall sore for seven days, 32and on the seventh day again examine the sore. If the scall has not spread and has no yellow hair on it and does not seem to have penetrated below the skin, 33the man shall shave himself, but not on the diseased spot. Then the priest shall quarantine him for another seven days. 34If the priest, when examining the scall on the seventh day, finds that it has not spread on the skin and that it has not penetrated below the skin, he shall declare the man clean; the latter shall wash his garments, and thus he will be clean. 35But if the scall spreads at all on his skin after he has been declared clean, 36the priest shall again examine it. If the scall has indeed spread on the skin, he need not look for yellow hair; the man is surely unclean. 37If, however, he judges that the scall has remained in its place and that black hair has grown on it, the disease has been healed; the man is clean, and the priest shall declare him clean.

38"When the skin of a man or a woman is spotted with white blotches, 39the priest shall make an examination. If the blotches on the skin are white and already dying out, it is only tetter that has broken out on the skin, and the person therefore is clean.

40"When a man loses the hair of his head, he is not unclean merely because of his bald crown. 41So too, if he loses the hair on the front of his head, he is not unclean merely because of his bald forehead. 42But when there is a pink sore on his bald crown or bald forehead, it is leprosy that is breaking out there. 43The priest shall examine him; and if the scab on the sore of the bald spot has the same pink appearance as that of skin leprosy of the fleshy part of the body, 44the man is leprous and unclean, and the priest shall declare him unclean by reason of the sore on his head.

45"The one who bears the sore of leprosy shall keep his garments rent and his head bare, and shall muffle his beard; he shall cry out, 'Unclean, unclean!' 46As long as the sore is on him he shall declare himself unclean, since he is in fact unclean. He shall dwell apart, making his abode outside the camp.

13:46 Living outside the camp. In some cases this means living alone. To live outside the camp came to be expressed as "outside the walls of the

Leprosy of Clothes. [47]"When a leprous infection is on a garment of wool or of linen, [48]or on woven or knitted material of linen or wool, or on a hide or anything made of leather, [49]if the infection on the garment or hide, or on the woven or knitted material, or on any leather article is greenish or reddish, the thing is indeed infected with leprosy and must be shown to the priest. [50]Having examined the infection, the priest shall quarantine the infected article for seven days.

[51]"On the seventh day the priest shall again examine the infection. If it has spread on the garment, or on the woven or knitted material, or on the leather, whatever be its use, the infection is malignant leprosy, and the article is unclean. [52]He shall therefore burn up the garment, or the woven or knitted material of wool or linen, or the leather article, whatever it may be, which is infected; since it has malignant leprosy, it must be destroyed by fire. [53]But if the priest, on examining the infection, finds that it has not spread on the garment, or on the woven or knitted material, or on the leather article, [54]he shall give orders to have the infected article washed and then quarantined for another seven days.

[55]"Then the priest shall again examine the infected article after it has been washed. If the infection has not changed its appearance, even though it may not have spread, the article is unclean and shall be destroyed by fire. [56]But if the priest, on examining the infection, finds that it is dying out after the washing, he shall tear the infected part out of the garment, or the leather, or the woven or knitted material. [57]If, however, the infection again appears on the garment, or on the woven or knitted material, or on the leather article, it is still virulent and the thing infected shall be destroyed by fire. [58]But if, after the washing, the infection has left the garment, or the woven or knitted material, or the leather article, the thing shall be washed a second time, and thus it will be clean. [59]This is the law for leprous infection on a garment of wool or linen, or on woven or knitted material, or on any leather article, to determine whether it is clean or unclean."

city," or sometimes in the case of temple regulations, "outside the temple mound," or in the wilderness, "outside the tabernacle community." One could come only to the entrance of the tent, as seen in chapters 12 and 15.

In view of the extensive treatment of skin disease in chapters 13 and 14, it seems that at the time there may have been an epidemic of unknown skin disorders. We do know without a doubt the importance of the blood as containing the life of every living body (17:11, 14). Today, the importance of a blood analysis is well-known as an indication of a person's general health. Likewise in Leviticus the slightest discoloration or bruise would need to be analyzed so that proper care would be taken to affirm the power of God in any flow of blood.

If we cut a finger, we know how easy it is to bring it to our mouth. The Hebrew word in the prohibition is "not to eat" (Lev 7:26; 17:10). Even though the prohibition may have had reference to some practice in the rituals of other peoples, its primary meaning should be considered as respect for life in recognition of the creator of life.

14 **Purification after Leprosy.** [1]The LORD said to Moses, [2]"This is the law for the victim of leprosy at the time of his purification. He shall be brought to the priest, [3]who is to go outside the camp to examine him. If the priest finds that the sore of leprosy has healed in the leper, [4]he shall order the man who is to be purified, to get two live, clean birds, as well as some cedar wood, scarlet yarn, and hyssop. [5]The priest shall then order him to slay one of the birds over an earthen vessel with spring water in it. [6]Taking the living bird with the cedar wood, the scarlet yarn and the hyssop, the priest shall dip them all in the blood of the bird that was slain over the spring water, [7]and then sprinkle seven times the

14:3 The priest goes outside the camp. The unclean person is not a part of the living community, but the priest can go to that person. However, to avoid defilement of the community, the priest must go outside to make his analysis. "Leprosy" here stands for any number of skin disorders.

14:4 The rite of purification. A vessel of fresh water is perhaps drawn from a spring or cistern by dipping clean pottery into the water. Fresh water is taken because the cleansing was outside the camp and its pure community. The blood from the one slain bird drips into the fresh water and receives proper care by contact with the water. The water can then be poured onto the ground and the vessel cleansed. The cedar wood (type used in the construction of the temple roof), scarlet yarn (blood color), and hyssop make a sprinkler. The hyssop is probably tied onto the cedar wood with the yarn. Everything is touched with the blood of the clean bird, for the life is in the blood. One of the birds stands for Israel (the afflicted person) about to reenter into the covenant relationship. The bird mediates the purification, since much of its life is spent flying between heaven and earth.

14:7 Purification through sevenfold sprinkling. Some references to sprinkling of the blood are found in Exod 12:22; 24:8; 29:21; Lev 4:6; 5:9, and reminds one of the Sinai Covenant. In fact, in Exod 24 the blood sprinkled on the altar and the people is called "the blood of the covenant." So now, at the renewal of the covenant, the blood is sprinkled. It is also a reminder of the Passover blood which freed the people from slavery. The slavery now is the skin disease, holding a person captive outside the camp.

In the ancient world, seven was a sacred number and considered a complete (holy) number. There were seven planets (five plus the sun and the moon) that had movement of their own among the fixed stars. Seven is one flanked by two groups of three; three was also a perfect number since it has a beginning, a middle, and an end (1-1-1). The sprinkling towards the Lord must be perfect, complete, holy; the sprinkling in atonement for the afflicted must also be complete (holy), since the skin infection is hardly ever in just one spot but in a number of different areas on the body. The purification must extend to the entire body of the leper; leaving one spot untouched would

man to be purified from his leprosy. When he has thus purified him, he shall let the living bird fly away over the countryside. ⁸The man being purified shall then wash his garments and shave off all his hair and bathe in water; only when he is thus made clean may he come inside the camp; but he shall still remain outside his tent for seven days. ⁹On the seventh day he shall again shave off all the hair of his head, his beard, his eye-brows, and any other hair he may have, and also wash his garments and bathe his body in water; and so he will be clean.

Purification Sacrifices. ¹⁰"On the eighth day he shall take two unblemished male lambs, one unblemished yearling ewe lamb, three tenths of an ephah of fine flour mixed with oil for a cereal offering, and one log of oil. ¹¹The priest who performs the purification

make the person unclean and further purification would be needed.

14:7 The second bird is set free. The bird is like the scapegoat, taking the leprosy away to a place of no return. Note the important ritual directive: one shall let the living bird fly away. First, the priest sprinkles the afflicted one. Then, as the purification takes place, one is handed the other bird. The purified one releases the (scape)bird. Thus the purification is completed. One can imagine the person feeling a real cleansing receiving the remaining bird from the priest and then releasing the infection along with the bird (a real carrier pigeon!) in the direction of the atoning God. Covenant life, wholeness, is restored for the individual with God and community. There is no question of magic, since the person is already healed when the rite of purification is performed (14:3). A parallel is the present-day rite of reconciliation, which deals with the leprosy of sin. The penitent approaches the rite of reconciliation, even though the sin is forgiven by an act of contrition. The priest mediates the sacramental (holy moment-um) ritual that affirms the forgiving and healing power of God present in the community and reconciles the person to the covenant-community relationship.

14:8 The one purified remains outside. One is inside the camp now, but outside the tent. This could mean outside the tabernacle or temple, since it was only on the eighth day that one was allowed to bring sacrifice into the temple.

14:9 The afflicted shaves again on the seventh day. The root ends of the hair have grown out and the ends of the defilement are cut off. The hair is cleansed and again washed. The reason may be more practical than symbolic, since by then a good decision can be made about the disorder.

14:10 The eighth-day offering. The ritual takes place in the temple. The ephah was about half a bushel, and a log was about two-thirds of a pint. The only type of offering not mentioned is the peace offering, since peace offerings were usually voluntary. The guilt offering would be required (see 5:14-26). Also, the one cleansed may have had to bring the guilt offering

ceremony shall place the man who is being purified, as well as all these offerings, before the LORD at the entrance of the meeting tent. ¹²Taking one of the male lambs, the priest shall present it as a guilt offering, along with the log of oil, waving them as a wave offering before the LORD. ¹³(This lamb he shall slaughter in the sacred place where the sin offering and the holocaust are slaughtered; because, like the sin offering, the guilt offering belongs to the priest and is most sacred.) ¹⁴Then the priest shall take some of the blood of the guilt offering and put it on the tip of the man's right ear, the thumb of his right hand, and the big toe of his right foot. ¹⁵The priest shall also take the log of oil and pour some of it into the palm of his own left hand; ¹⁶then, dipping his right forefinger in it, he shall sprinkle it seven times before the LORD. ¹⁷Of the oil left in his hand the priest shall put some on the tip of the man's right ear, the thumb of his right

to make up for the absenteeism from temple ritual during the time of being cut off.

14:12-13 The wave offering. This action might better be described as a "lifting up" rather than a wave offering. Perhaps this is the lifting up of one's hands in the manner of the priest today at the offering of the bread and wine. It could refer to praying with hands lifted up. In any case the Hebrew word is related to the English "height." Verse 13 refers to the guilt offering as "most sacred," since the wholeness of every member of the covenant is affirmed.

14:14 Blood put on the tip of one's ear, thumb, and big toe. The ancients believed that access to one's life by spirits was made through these extremities—as in the case of unclean (5:2) or sacred (6:11). Blood was used to cleanse and to ward off the unclean or evil. Later we shall see the anointing over the blood with oil. This anointing would seemingly prepare for the purification and entrance of the good spirit. Today, during baptism, the tip of the ear and the mouth are touched in preparation for receiving and speaking the word of God.

In the ordination rite of the priest, the blood of the ordination ram is splashed on the altar (Exod 29:19-25 and Lev 8–9). The priest is consecrated to the Lord. The altar splashing is not mentioned here, since it is the guilt offering of lamb's blood that is sprinkled seven times before the Lord. A change in the direction of the ritual action, or the omission of a particular rite where one might expect it to be repeated, may indicate a meaning of the present ritual. Thus, every area of life can be covered with positive regulation. However, the precision of the Levitical regulation seems to make some readers shy away from these Torah instructions. But to others this precision offers an exciting treasure hunt.

14:17 Oil over the blood of the guilt offering. Putting the oil over the blood signifies the complete return to covenant life. The oil represents God

hand, and the big toe of his right foot, over the blood of the guilt offering. [18]The rest of the oil in his hand the priest shall put on the head of the man being purified. Thus shall the priest make atonement for him before the LORD. [19]Only after he has offered the sin offering in atonement for the man's uncleanness shall the priest slaughter the holocaust [20]and offer it, together with the cereal offering, on the altar before the LORD. When the priest has thus made atonement for him, the man will be clean.

Poor Leper's Sacrifice. [21]"If a man is poor and cannot afford so much, he shall take one male lamb for a guilt offering, to be used as a wave offering in atonement for himself, one tenth of an ephah of fine flour mixed with oil for a cereal offering, a log of oil, [22]and two turtledoves or pigeons, which he can more easily afford, the one as a sin offering and the other as a holocaust. [23]On the eighth day of his purification he shall bring them to the priest, at the entrance of the meeting tent before the LORD. [24]Taking the guilt-offering lamb, along with the log of oil, the priest shall wave them as a wave offering before the LORD. [25]When he has slaughtered the guilt-offering lamb, he shall take some of its blood, and put it on the tip of the right ear of the man being purified, on the thumb of his right hand, and on the big toe of his right foot. [26]The priest shall then pour some of the oil into the palm of his own left hand [27]and with his right forefinger sprinkle it seven times before the LORD. [28]Some of the oil in his hand the priest shall also put on the tip of the man's right ear, the thumb of his right hand, and the big toe of his right foot, over the blood of the guilt offering. [29]The rest of the oil in his hand the priest shall put on the man's head. Thus shall he make atonement for him before the LORD. [30]Then, of the turtledoves or pigeons, such as the man can afford, [31]the priest shall offer up one as a sin offering and the other as a holocaust, along with the cereal offering. Thus shall the priest make atonement before the LORD for the man who is to be purified. [32]This is the law for one afflicted with leprosy who has insufficient means for his purification."

Leprosy of Houses. [33]The LORD said to Moses and Aaron, [34]"When you come into the land of Canaan, which I am giving you to possess, if I put a leprous infection on any house of the land you oc-

at work in the individual and community life of the people. God gives life to the blood relationship. For a priest needing such purification, this ritual acts as a mini reconsecration rite (see also 8:10). The covenant is renewed and all are ready for the life of holiness with its enduring and maturing obedience, purification, and holy conduct.

14:21 A poor leper's sacrifice. The reduced requirement of turtledoves rather than lambs makes the purification ritual easier on the poor. The emphasis is on the recognition of the covenant, not on the requirement of the offering. However, the requirement of the guilt offering seems to have remained the same for all, since the affirmation of both God and neighbor is involved. The same requirement for everyone openly expresses this involvement, even though the guilty party acted unwillingly or inadvertently (5:14-26).

14:33-57 Cleansing the houses. Like the individual in need of cleansing and purification, so the dwelling place of the individual. Recall that even

cupy, [35]the owner of the house shall come and report to the priest, 'It looks to me as if my house were infected.' [36]The priest shall then order the house to be cleared out before he goes in to examine the infection, lest everything in the house become unclean. Only after this is he to go in to examine the house. [37]If the priest, on examining it, finds that the infection on the walls of the house consists of greenish or reddish depressions which seem to go deeper than the surface of the wall, [38]he shall close the door of the house behind him and quarantine the house for seven days. [39]On the seventh day the priest shall return to examine the house again. If he finds that the infection has spread on the walls, [40]he shall order the infected stones to be pulled out and cast in an unclean place outside the city. [41]The whole inside of the house shall then be scraped, and the mortar that has been scraped off shall be dumped in an unclean place outside the city. [42]Then new stones shall be brought and put in the place of the old stones, and new mortar shall be made and plastered on the house.

[43]"If the infection breaks out once more after the stones have been pulled out and the house has been scraped and replastered, [44]the priest shall come again; and if he finds that the infection has spread in the house, it is corrosive leprosy, and the house in unclean. [45]It shall be pulled down, and all its stones, beams and mortar shall be hauled away to an unclean place outside the city. [46]Whoever enters a house while it is quarantined shall be unclean until evening. [47]Whoever sleeps or eats in such a house shall also wash his garments. [48]If the priest finds, when he comes to examine the house, that the infection has in fact not spread after the plastering, he shall declare the house clean, since the infection has been healed. [49]To purify the house, he shall take two birds, as well as cedar wood, scarlet yarn, and hyssop. [50]One of the birds he shall slay over an earthen vessel with spring water in it. [51]Then, taking the cedar wood, the hyssop and the scarlet yarn, together with the living bird, he shall dip them all in the blood of the slain bird and the spring water, and sprinkle the house seven times. [52]Thus shall he purify the house with the bird's blood and the spring water, along with the living bird, the cedar wood, the hyssop, and the scarlet yarn. [53]He shall then let the living bird fly away over the countryside out-

the dwelling place of the Lord was in need of purification from time to time. On the Day of Atonement there was purification of every possible defilement that could have occurred throughout the previous year (16:16-19).

14:37 "Infection on the walls . . ." This seems to be mold and rust, but in view of verse 34 and in the opinion of some rabbis, it was considered a defilement sent in punishment for one's lack of faith. Mold and rust assured that some type of life must be present. Therefore, a regulation had to ensure proper recognition of the source of life and respect for the life itself.

Some types of defilement are unavoidable or accidental, and some occur even in the normal course of events (recurrent body flows and sickness). Some can happen while performing commendable acts (Lev 16:21-28; Num 19:7, 8, 10). The rabbis call these "defilements of the body."

The rabbis thought that sin occurs when the unclean and the holy, or the clean and the profane, are brought together in a spirit of disobedience—for example, the entry into the Holy Place by one forbidden to do so or eating

side the city. When he has thus made atonement for it, the house will be clean.

⁵⁴"This is the law for every kind of human leprosy and scall, ⁵⁵for leprosy of garments and houses, ⁵⁶as well as for scabs, pustules and blotches, ⁵⁷so that it may be manifest when there is a state of uncleanness and when a state of cleanness. This is the law for leprosy."

15 **Personal Uncleanness.** ¹The LORD said to Moses and Aaron, ²"Speak to the Israelites and tell them: Every man who is afflicted with a chronic flow from his private parts is thereby unclean. ³Such is his uncleanness from this flow that it makes no difference whether the flow drains off or is blocked up; his uncleanness remains. ⁴Any bed on which the man afflicted with the flow lies, is unclean, and any piece of furniture on which he sits, is unclean. ⁵Anyone who touches his bed shall wash his garments, bathe in water, and be unclean until evening. ⁶Whoever sits on a piece of furniture on which the afflicted man was sitting, shall wash his garments, bathe in water, and be unclean until evening. ⁷Whoever touches the body of the afflicted man shall wash his garments, bathe in water, and be unclean until evening. ⁸If the afflicted man spits on a clean man, the latter shall wash his garments, bathe in water, and be unclean until evening. ⁹Any saddle on which the afflicted man rides, is unclean. ¹⁰Whoever touches anything that was under him shall be unclean until evening; whoever lifts up any such thing shall wash his garments,

bathe in water, and be unclean until evening. ¹¹Anyone whom the afflicted man touches with unrinsed hands shall wash his garments, bathe in water, and be unclean until evening. ¹²Earthenware touched by the afflicted man shall be broken; and every wooden article shall be rinsed with water.

¹³"When a man who has been afflicted with a flow becomes free of his affliction, he shall wait seven days for his purification. Then he shall wash his garments and bathe his body in fresh water, and so he will be clean. ¹⁴On the eighth day he shall take two turtledoves or two pigeons, and going before the LORD, to the entrance of the meeting tent, he shall give them to the priest, ¹⁵who shall offer them up, the one as a sin offering and the other as a holocaust. Thus shall the priest make atonement before the LORD for the man's flow.

¹⁶"When a man has an emission of seed, he shall bathe his whole body in water and be unclean until evening. ¹⁷Any piece of cloth or leather with seed on it shall be washed with water and be unclean until evening.

¹⁸"If a man lies carnally with a woman, they shall both bathe in water and be unclean until evening.

¹⁹"When a woman has her menstrual flow, she shall be in a state of impurity for seven days. Anyone who touches her shall be unclean until evening. ²⁰Anything on which she lies or sits during her impurity shall be unclean. ²¹Anyone who touches her bed shall wash his garments, bathe in water, and be unclean until evening. ²²Whoever

clean food while one is in an unclean state. Obedience is still the key in a covenant relationship. God is the only one who can say, "I am the Lord."

Obedience is the key to purification and holiness. It may seem that the Book of Leviticus speaks only of *ritual* obedience, but the Code of Holiness points to the necessity of obedience in the *whole* of life. Lev 1–7 concern obedience. Chapters 11–15 express the purification that results from obedience. Then, and only then, will one begin to live a holy life.

15:13 One is to bathe in fresh water. Cleanliness contains a twofold idea: first, to be healed of a disease or purified from uncleanness (see 14:48,

touches any article of furniture on which she was sitting, shall wash his garments, bathe in water, and be unclean until evening. 23But if she is on the bed or on the seat when he touches it, he shall be unclean until evening. 24If a man dares to lie with her, he contracts her impurity and shall be unclean for seven days; every bed on which he then lies also becomes unclean.

25"When a woman is afflicted with a flow of blood for several days outside her menstrual period, or when her flow continues beyond the ordinary period, as long as she suffers this unclean flow she shall be unclean, just as during her menstrual period. 26Any bed on which she lies during such a flow becomes unclean, as it would during her menstruation, and any article of furniture on which she sits becomes unclean just as during her menstruation. 27Anyone who touches them becomes unclean; he shall wash his garments, bathe in water, and be unclean until evening.

28"If she becomes freed from her affliction, she shall wait seven days, and only then is she to be purified. 29On the eighth day she shall take two turtledoves or two pigeons and bring them to the priest at the entrance of the meeting tent. 30The priest shall offer up one of them as a sin offering and the other as a holocaust. Thus shall the priest make atonement before the Lord for her unclean flow.

31"You shall warn the Israelites of their uncleanness, lest by defiling my Dwelling, which is in their midst, their uncleanness be the cause of their death.

32"This is the law for the man who is afflicted with a chronic flow, or who has an emission of seed, and thereby becomes unclean; 33as well as for the woman who has her menstrual period, or who is afflicted with a chronic flow; the law for male and female; and also for the man who lies with an unclean woman."

16 **The Day of Atonement.** 1After the death of Aaron's two sons,

49), and second, washed (in some cases, bathing in a stream or fresh-water lake, or whatever assigned regulation) to establish the purification. The process is a mini-freedom from Egypt leading into the Promised Land.

16:1-34 The Day of Atonement. This chapter has a unique place in Leviticus because it acts as a bridge connecting the rite of purification and the life of holiness (chs. 17–26). It is the Lord who initiates the atonement. The Lord does this by demanding the purification of the Holy of Holies, which has been defiled by the deaths of Nadab and Abihu.

Then the rite of sanctuary purification is joined with the confession and removal of the sins of both priests and people (16:33). This latter purification takes place in what is called the scapegoat ritual. This joint celebration, along with the mortification of fasting (vv. 29-31), begins the life of holiness. On the Day of Atonement, the sanctuary and the nation celebrate the atonement feast.

16:1 Purification after the death of Nadab and Abihu. This is the place to refer again to chapter 10, since it sets the stage for sanctuary purification. Here is a known defilement of the sanctuary. Their corpses made the Holy of Holies unclean and in need of purification. Perhaps they had gotten too close to the propitiatory (seat of mercy) on the ark. There were certain regulations for making a proper entry into the Holy of Holies. Note how the first span of the bridge to holiness is contructed from some leftover material of

who died when they approached the Lord's presence, the Lord spoke to Moses [2]and said to him, "Tell your brother Aaron that he is not to come whenever he pleases into the sanctuary, inside the veil, in front of the propitiatory on the ark; otherwise, when I reveal myself in a cloud above the propitiatory, he will die. [3]Only in this way may Aaron enter the sanctuary. He shall bring a young bullock for a sin offering and a ram for a holocaust. [4]He shall wear the sacred linen tunic, with the linen drawers next his flesh, gird himself with the linen sash and put on the linen miter. But since these vestments are sacred, he shall not put them on until he has first bathed his body in water. [5]From the Israelite community he shall receive two male goats for a sin offering and one ram for a holocaust.

[6]"Aaron shall bring in the bullock, his sin offering to atone for himself and for his household. [7]Taking the two male goats, and setting them before the Lord at the entrance of the meeting tent, [8]he shall cast lots to determine which one is for the Lord and which for Azazel. [9]The goat that is determined by lot for the Lord, Aaron shall bring in and offer up as a sin offering. [10]But the goat determined by lot for Azazel he shall set alive before the Lord, so that with it he may make atonement by sending it off to Azazel in the desert.

[11]"Thus shall Aaron offer up the bullock, his sin offering, to atone for himself and for his family. When he has slaughtered it, [12]he shall take a censer full of glowing embers from the altar before the Lord, as well as a double handful of finely ground fragrant incense, and bringing them inside the veil, [13]there before the Lord he shall put incense on the fire, so that a cloud of incense may cover the propitiatory over the commandments; else he will die. [14]Taking some of the bullock's blood, he shall sprinkle it with his finger on the fore part of the propitiatory and likewise sprinkle some of the blood with his finger seven times in front of the propitiatory.

[15]"Then he shall slaughter the people's sin-offering goat, and bringing its blood inside the veil, he shall do with it as he did with the bullock's blood, sprinkling it on the propitiatory and before it. [16]Thus he shall make atonement for the sanctuary because of all the sinful defilements and faults of the Israelites. He shall do the same for the meeting tent, which is set up among them in the midst of their uncleanness. [17]No one else may be in the meeting tent from the time he enters the sanctuary to make atonement

chapters 11–15 and reaching back into chapter 10. This first span is set in place. God and nation are ready to obey the order of purification.

16:2-5 The propitiatory on the ark. This is the mercy seat of the Lord. The place of at-one-ment must be at the mercy seat of the Lord. It is the cover over the ark containing the Ten Commandments. The cleansing of the sanctuary with its consequent purification is now able to take place here. In Hebrew the very word for *cover* is related to the word for *atonement*. It means that the guilt is covered over or that atonement is payment for being reinstated.

16:3-21 The rite of purification. The gold and white vestments are interchanged, signifying the presence of God and the people at work together. Mutually they take part in the atonement action that removes all the defilement of the past year, even that which may have happened inadvertently. Together in the life of holiness a new year is begun for God and people (chs. 17–27).

until he departs. When he has made atonement for himself and his household, as well as for the whole Israelite community, ¹⁸he shall come out to the altar before the LORD and make atonement for it also. Taking some of the bullock's and the goat's blood, he shall put it on the horns around the altar, ¹⁹and with his finger sprinkle some of the blood on it seven times. Thus he shall render it clean and holy, purged of the defilements of the Israelites.

The Scapegoat. ²⁰"When he has completed the atonement rite for the sanctuary, the meeting tent and the altar, Aaron shall bring forward the live goat. ²¹Laying both hands on its head, he shall confess over it all the sinful faults and transgressions of the Israelites, and so put them on the goat's head. He shall then have it led into the desert by an at-tendant. ²²Since the goat is to carry off their iniquities to an isolated region, it must be sent away into the desert.

²³"After Aaron has again gone into the meeting tent, he shall strip off and leave in the sanctuary the linen vestments he had put on when he entered there. ²⁴After bathing his body with water in a sacred place, he shall put on his vestments, and then come out and offer his own and the people's holocaust, in atonement for himself and for the people, ²⁵and also burn the fat of the sin offering on the altar.

²⁶"The man who has led away the goat for Azazel shall wash his garments and bathe his body in water; only then may he enter the camp. ²⁷The sin-offering bullock and goat whose blood was brought into the sanctuary to make atonement, shall be taken outside the

So, this atonement chapter acts as the bridge where the two members of the covenant (God and the people) come together to celebrate the at-oneness to be experienced in the Code of Holiness.

16:20-28 The scapegoat ritual: means of atonement. There are actually two goats and a ram for a holocaust. One goat is offered as a sin offering. By the laying on of hands, the other receives the sins of the community and is sent to carry them off to a place of no return. Azazel (perhaps "power of El") seems to be a wordplay on the subduing of a foreign god (demon).

One goat represents the action of the purification of the sanctuary (v. 20). The other represents the atonement of the people in what has come to be known as a scapegoat ritual. The goat is driven into the desert, the place of no return and also the place of "just desert." This latter wordplay on desert alters the entire meaning of the word.

With the additional span of removal and punishment complete, the bridge-chapter furthers its construction towards covenant renewal.

During the ritual Aaron changes from gold to white, back to gold, and to white again. Before and after each change there are ritual bathings. God and people are represented in the vestments. Ritual directs the priest to dress up in different costumes to portray different characters. The simple white lines were also a sign of humility and honest contrition flowing between the two members of the covenant. Actions like the vestment changing (16:4, 23, 24, 32) pave the way for the atonement that is in progress.

Today Yom Kippur or the Day of Atonement is celebrated with great faith in the at-one-ment of God and people. It is a very important day for

camp, where their hides and flesh and offal shall be burned up in the fire. ²⁸The one who burns them shall wash his garments and bathe his body in water; only then may he enter the camp.

The Fast. ²⁹"This shall be an everlasting ordinance for you: on the tenth day of the seventh month every one of you, whether a native or a resident alien, shall mortify himself and shall do no work. ³⁰Since on this day atonement is made for you to make you clean, so that you may be cleansed of all your sins before the LORD, ³¹by everlasting ordinance it shall be a most solemn sab-

bath for you, on which you must mortify yourselves.

³²"This atonement is to be made by the priest who has been anointed and ordained to the priesthood in succession to his father. He shall wear the linen garments, the sacred vestments, ³³and make atonement for the sacred sanctuary, the meeting tent and the altar, as well as for the priests and all the people of the community. ³⁴This, then, shall be an everlasting ordinance for you: once a year atonement shall be made for all the sins of the Israelites."

Thus was it done, as the LORD had commanded Moses.

the Jew who seeks reconciliation with other members of the community and then receives atonement from God (see also Matt 5:24). One of the readings of the Jewish atonement celebration today is Isa 57:14–58:14, which speaks of a real inner, moral renewal by fasting (Lev 16:29-31). Fasting is made genuine by going out to others, especially the poor and the unfortunate, and by concentrating on a change of life for all (vv. 29, 30). In Leviticus all are now ready for the change to a life of holiness.

PART IV: CODE OF LEGAL HOLINESS

Lev 17–26

This section in Leviticus emphasizes life more than ritual, but obedience to the command of God is still at work. The covenant arrangement is still to be preserved (17:2). God is to be recognized first (v. 4). If this is not carried out, one is to be cut off from those who wish to keep this life-covenant arrangement (v. 4). It is a whole new way of life (v. 5-7). What is presented in the Code of Holiness (17–26) is for everyone (v. 8). We need to be in touch with regulations that have gone before, but we cannot forget the practice of obedience, and the bridge (Lev 16) must be kept intact (17:2, 4, 9). Obedience is still at work now, with emphasis on principle rather than regulation. It is this change that seems to encourage more people to read this section of Leviticus rather than chapters 1–16, which stress ritual obedience. Ritual conformity, practiced only for the sake of obedience, becomes a very heavy burden in time. However, obedience, along with purification, is required in order to be fully alive in the life of holiness. Now the obedience is to a lifestyle embodied in the Code of Holiness.

The difference between "sacrifice" and "sanctification" should be noted. Sacrifice is the "making holy" and sanctification can be the "living holy"of life. One's living-out of purification (chs. 11–16) through obedience (chs. 1–7) opens the way to sanctification (chs. 17–27).

We now come to the very beat of the heart in the Code of Holiness (chs. 17–27). "Be holy, for I, the Lord, your God, am holy." Even the flow of the accent in this English quotation of the central theme (19:2) has a pulsating rhythm.

These chapters offer directives for living a life of holiness. They were guidelines for the people of old as they are for the people of today.

We accept, then, the real life situation of our ancestors and rejoice in their liturgical activity, whatever the expression. We can imagine the closeness they had with life and death; their struggle with the animals being dragged to the entrance of the meeting tent or temple; the shame, exposure, inconvenience, and humiliation of being people who had to keep at a distance at a time when community care and support was so needed and who were obliged to call out, "Unclean, Unclean!" (13:45). What a variety of offertory processions to the Holy One! Then came the slaughter, with the spurting, sprinkling and smearing of blood, and the smell covered over by incense. Like a grand finale, the cloud suggested that the sounds of sin and death were then transformed into a chorus of praise of the presence of God in the midst of the people (26:11-13). One can almost hear the ram's horn (shofar) and the soothing sound of the lute that are now silent. There may be a certain "away from home" feeling in the hearts of all people today, but the holy message of Leviticus is alive and pulsating, in the expectation and excitement of the Holy One, the Messiah-Redeemer, who is to establish the everlasting dwelling place (Ps 43:3).

Here we are given laws, directives, morals, and morale that beat and pulsate to real life situations. Lev 26 will put the finishing touches on the covenant arrangement by detailing the rewards of obedience and the punishments of disobedience—specifics usually included in a covenant treaty. They were both an incentive and a scare tactic to assert the dominion of the king over the subject and to encourage the subject to follow the commands of the king.

Chapter 17. Scholars have discussed whether or not this chapter is a part of the Code of Holiness. Some think that chapter 17 acts as a bridge over all the material *preceding* the Code of Holiness, since there is mention of the offerings of Lev 1–3 as a prelude to Lev 18:5. There God is recognized as the source of the command to be fully alive.

The people were commanded to bring everything to the entrance of the meeting tent to be offered to the Lord (Lev 1:3, 2:2, 3:2, and corresponding

IV: CODE OF LEGAL HOLINESS

17 **Sacredness of Blood.** [1]The LORD said to Moses, [2]"Speak to Aaron and his sons, as well as to all the Israelites, and tell them: This is what the LORD has commanded. [3]Any Israelite who slaughters an ox or a sheep or a goat, whether in the camp or outside of it, [4]without first bringing it to the entrance of the meeting tent to present it as an offering to the LORD in front of his Dwelling, shall be judged guilty of bloodshed; and for this, such a man shall be cut off from among his people. [5]Therefore, such sacrifices as they used to offer up in the open field the Israelites shall henceforth offer to the LORD, bringing them to the priest at the entrance of the meeting tent and sacrificing them there as peace offerings to the LORD. [6]The priest shall splash the blood on the altar of the LORD at the entrance of the meeting tent and there burn the fat for an odor pleasing to the LORD. [7]No longer shall they offer their sacrifices to the satyrs to whom they used to render their wanton worship. This shall be an ever-

to these commands are 17:4, 5, and 6). The priesthood (chs. 8–10) and purification (chs. 11–16) also parallel chapter 17. Because of these features, chapter 17 seems to assume a fitting role as the introduction to the Code of Holiness. The chapter could even have been an addition to the original little "Manual of Holiness." But we see more reason to accept chapter 17 as the original first chapter of the Manual of Holiness. The preceding chapters 1–16 could be expanded ideas, practices, and traditions of the original Code of Holiness.

In Lev 1–7 the emphasis was on obedience, simply because God commanded obedience. Chapter 17 gives reason why a person is to obey, and the command to obey assumes fuller import in the covenant relationship.

17:3, 8, 13, 15 The sacredness of blood. Everyone is commanded to recognize the source of life in the one, holy God. By respecting the life that is in the blood and acting out this respect through the ritual of putting the blood on the altar (17:11), the atonement (at-one-ment) of the people's lives is effected. The text says that the blood, as the seat of life, makes the atonement. This is interesting and understandable, since the presence of the Lord is believed to reside over the seat of mercy that covers the ark in the Holy of Holies. God, the source of life, is hidden in the blood, and the sin of the people is now hidden or covered by the atoning presence of God (16:13).

The Code of Holiness will be issued in chapter 18. It is an invitation to the human-divine marriage (18:5)—to partake of the fruit of the tree of life, to eat of it, and live forever the life of holiness. The final chapter of Leviticus will hint at the everlasting character of this life.

First, we have a final comment concerning the respect and use of blood. Many regulations concerning the blood were wrapped in the fate of the lifeblood of the bleeding animal. While Western thought tends to spiritualize life and reality (in the sense of constructing an ideal world) and to speak of death as disturbing proper order, for the biblical people everything was

lasting ordinance for them and their descendants.

⁸"Tell them, therefore: Anyone, whether of the house of Israel or of the aliens residing among them, who offers a holocaust or sacrifice ⁹without bringing it to the entrance of the meeting tent to offer it to the LORD, shall be cut off from his kinsmen. ¹⁰And if anyone, whether of the house of Israel or of the aliens residing among them, partakes of any blood, I will set myself against that one who partakes of blood and will cut him off from among his people. ¹¹Since the life of a living body is in its blood, I have made you put it on the altar, so that atonement may thereby be made for your own lives, because it is the blood, as the seat of life, that makes atonement. ¹²That is why I have told the Israelites: No one among you, not even a resident alien, may partake of blood.

¹³"Anyone hunting, whether of the Israelites or of the aliens residing among them, who catches an animal or a bird that may be eaten, shall pour out its blood and cover it with earth. ¹⁴Since the life of every living body is its blood, concrete. Blood was life, and the pouring out of blood was death, and death acted as a thief stealing life.

To be able to think as did the writers of Sacred Scriptures is crucial to understanding the Bible. The biblical people thought and expressed themselves in concrete terms. Since God chose to use this medium for the Divine Word to enter into the world, we need to be aware of this way of thinking.

For the Hebrew mind the Word of God was real, spoken as real as the greeting exchanged between neighbors ("The Lord spoke to Moses . . . , and from the meeting tent gave him this message . . ."). The life of the ancient Hebrews was lived in the presence of God. The language of Scripture reflects a people who thought, lived, and moved in a real world, and their God was very much a part of the real world. Their expression of what God had to say was also real. Truth, justice, and peace were not ideas, but living things. For the Hebrew, "Kindness and truth shall meet; justice and peace shall kiss. Truth shall spring out of the earth, and justice shall look down from heaven" (Ps 85:11-12).

Also, every slaughter of an animal, even if just for food, had to be a sacrifice (a making holy) or a sanctification (a living holy), since the animal victim enabled the offerer to continue living. God, the source of life, had to be recognized in some way. Thus when people were no longer in proximity to the altar, the first regulation of putting the blood on the altar was modified (Deut 12:24). It was to be poured out on the ground like water and could then return to the Lord.

17:13 The blood of the clean animal. In the case of a clean animal killed while hunting, the blood was to be buried. Similarly, a scribe who erred in copying the Sacred Scripture did not crumple the page and start over. Rather, he carefully extracted the infected portion of the scroll (as in a surgical procedure), encased it in a little casket, and buried it (as in a funeral). As the life is in the blood (v. 14), so the Spirit of Holiness is in the Holy Word.

I have told the Israelites: You shall not partake of the blood of any meat. Since the life of every living body is its blood, anyone who partakes of it shall be cut off. ¹⁵Everyone, whether a native or an alien, who eats of an animal that died of itself or was killed by a wild beast, shall wash his garments, bathe in water, and be unclean until evening, and then he will be clean. ¹⁶If he does not wash or does not bathe his body, he shall have the guilt to bear."

18 **The Sanctity of Sex.** ¹The LORD said to Moses, ²"Speak to the Israelites and tell them: I, the LORD, am your God. ³You shall not do as they do in the land of Egypt, where you once lived, nor shall you do as they do in the land of Canaan, where I am bringing you; do not conform to their customs. ⁴My decrees you shall carry out, and my statutes you shall take care to follow. I, the LORD, am your God. ⁵Keep, then, my statutes and decrees, for the man who carries them out will find life through them. I am the LORD.

⁶"None of you shall approach a close relative to have sexual intercourse with her. I am the LORD. ⁷You shall not disgrace your father by having intercourse with your mother. Besides, since she is your own mother, you shall not have intercourse with her. ⁸You shall not have intercourse with your father's wife, for that would be a disgrace to your father. ⁹You shall not have intercourse with your sister, your father's daughter or your mother's daughter, whether she was born in your own household or born elsewhere. ¹⁰You shall not have intercourse with your son's daughter or with your daughter's daughter, for that would be a disgrace to your own family. ¹¹You shall not have intercourse with the daughter whom your father's wife bore to him, since she, too, is your sister. ¹²You shall not have intercourse with your father's sister, since she is your father's relative. ¹³You shall not have intercourse with your mother's sister, since she is your mother's relative. ¹⁴You shall not disgrace your father's brother by being intimate with his wife, since she, too,

Even though the putting of the blood on the altar was later modified in Deuteronomy and is not possible today (the temple was destroyed by the Romans in A.D. 70), the prohibition of eating blood has remained in Jewish practice to this day. The regulation could be changed only if God, the source of life, would invite people to eat the blood. So, the command would then be, "Eat my blood," which, in Hebrew thought would be, "Become one with my life."

18:1-30 The sanctity of sex. It follows from the affirmation of the source of life that any control over that life would need to follow the order (command) of the source of life. Covenant relation concerning life demands that the lesser partner (creature) takes direction (life and order) from the greater or source-partner (creator). Holiness in the control of life (sex) is to be found in the ordering which accords with God's plan. Not only does one have life (18:5) but one can also share in the control of life (18:3). This is the reason for the constant reminder that God is the source of life, "I am the Lord." The only authentic plan of living (Code of Holiness) is the plan of the "God who is" (Yahweh). Thus, the writer begins chapter 18 with the Lord saying to Moses, "Speak to the Israelites and tell them: I, the Lord, am your God" (v. 2). One can hear this beat of the heart of the Torah in 18:2-6, 21, 30;

is your aunt. ¹⁵You shall not have intercourse with your daughter-in-law; she is your son's wife, and therefore you shall not disgrace her. ¹⁶You shall not have intercourse with your brother's wife, for that would be a disgrace to your brother. ¹⁷You shall not have intercourse with a woman and also with her daughter, nor shall you marry and have intercourse with her son's daughter or her daughter's daughter; this would be shameful, because they are related to her. ¹⁸While your wife is still living you shall not marry her sister as her rival; for thus you would disgrace your first wife. ¹⁹"You shall not approach a woman to have intercourse with her while she is unclean from menstruation. ²⁰You shall not have carnal relations with your neighbor's wife, defiling yourself with her. ²¹You shall not offer any of your offspring to be immolated to Molech, thus profaning the name of your God. I am the LORD. ²²You shall not lie with a male as with a woman; such a thing is an abomination. ²³You shall not have carnal relations with an animal, defiling yourself with it; nor shall a woman set herself in front of an animal to mate with it; such things are abhorrent.

²⁴"Do not defile yourselves by any of these things by which the nations whom I am driving out of your way have defiled themselves. ²⁵Because their land has

19:2, 4, 10, 11, 13, 15, and elsewhere. Life is found by following God's plan (v. 5).

18:18 A bridge-verse. In the language of regulation the word sex stands for both male and female, even though each has a unique sharing in the control of the one life of God.

Verse 18 is a bridge-verse. It connects a list of incest prohibitions with a list of other "out-of-order" sexual relations. Lev 18:6-17 lists the disorderly acts of incest; then verse 18 says, "While your wife is still living, you shall not marry her sister as her rival; for thus you would disgrace your first wife." The second part of the verse refers to the disorder created in the life plan of God (in the Hebrew, Yah-God is mentioned as joined to the very life of the wife). This part also acts as a bridge to all the other disorders or immoral relations that are prohibited (vv. 19-23). The disorder implied in the first part of verse 18 results because a man already united to a woman violates the covenant arrangement, marries his sister-in-law, and creates a polygamous relationship. This disorder relates to incest and affects the community in which all, including the sister, should live the same holy life. The first part of the verse connects as a bridge to prohibitions of incest; the "disgrace" connects with other community disorders.

One should notice, for the sake of completeness, that the incest of father and daughter should not even have to be mentioned, but it is included in verse 6 and is accorded one of the pulsating phrases, "I am the Lord." In verse 22 the disorder is called an abomination, which in Hebrew means trying to make holy a union that cannot be completed in the real sense of the action. This is the reason why it is usually referred to as making a sacrifice to a strange god. The ordering of the source of life and the orderly plan of God within the covenant is cut off.

become defiled, I am punishing it for its wickedness, by making it vomit out its inhabitants. [26]You, however, whether natives or resident aliens, must keep my statutes and decrees forbidding all such abominations [27]by which the previous inhabitants defiled the land; [28]otherwise the land will vomit you out also for hav-ing defiled it, just as it vomited out the nations before you. [29]Everyone who does any of these abominations shall be cut off from among his people. [30]Heed my charge, then, not to defile yourselves by observing the abominable customs that have been observed before you. I, the LORD, am your God."

When the marriage invitation in chapter 18 is accepted by both parties of the covenant, the holy life takes on the renewed dimension of oneness along with completeness. To be at one in the Lord is the goal of the divine-human covenant.

In chapter 19 we need to be careful not to read into the text more or less than the writer or editors intended.

In chapters 17–26, the Code of Holiness (H), some material has vocabulary and unity of its own and is recognized by scholars as having a very early date. It, too, centers around the call of Israel to be holy. This Code may have been the core around which the final editors gathered other Priestly material. For these reasons this section is often referred to by the letter H. Ritual regulations are absent, and the text begins to talk in terms of principle and conduct. The tone is more ethical than ritual. The reader may feel more at home in this section of Leviticus. Here we have directives for living a holy life. Echoes of Genesis and Exodus commands are heard in the regulations of the Code of Holiness. For Adam and Eve in Gen 1:28, for Noah and family after the flood in Gen 8:17 and 9:7, and for all the people in Exod 20, "Eat and multiply," is the directive, "but do not divide by defilement for I, the Lord, am your God."

19:1-37 Various rules of conduct. The two basic rules of the divine-human relationship are found here—love of God and love of neighbor. That this twofold directive is alive and breathing today is witness enough to its enduring validity. Verses 2 and 18 give the commands "Be holy, for I, the Lord, your God, am holy" and "You shall love your neighbor as yourself."

In 20:1-8 and 20:9-21, the respective penalties are given for disobeying these commands. The remaining verses of chapter 20 spell out, in no uncertain terms, what will happen to the disobedient. In other words, ethically as well as ritually, the covenant relationship is still founded on obedience. This is a basic tenet of the covenant agreement and points to a proper order. Obedience to the order of covenant relations is the basis of accepting the rules of the life of holiness. The important question is not "Who's on first?" but "Who comes first?" Often we may think that holiness is achieved by giving up some part of life or by depriving one member of the covenant. However,

19 **Various Rules of Conduct.** ¹The LORD said to Moses, ²"Speak to the whole Israelite community and tell them: Be holy, for I, the LORD, your God, am holy. ³Revere your mother and father, and keep my sabbaths. I, the

to submit to the superior member of the covenant is the basic meaning of a covenant treaty.

The negative directives of chapter 18 were issued because at various times the people had taken direction contrary to the plan of holiness. Often, in assessing guilt, it is not the good or evil of the action that needs to be considered, but rather the order or manner of its performance. Examples abound in chapter 18. Intercourse is not forbidden in itself. What is forbidden are the disorderly situations that are contrary to the Code of Holiness and the life-giving power of the Creator.

What seems to be given as a penalty—the "vomiting of the people out of the land"—is simply a stated result of disorderly conduct similar to what happens in the case of a social stomach disorder. In chapter 26 we find that God, as the source of life, uses time itself to retrieve the divine order from the disorder caused by the human member of the covenant. This is an aspect of the everlasting covenant—God still gives us time to live and sustains us in life even when we choose to make fools of ourselves or even when we cut ourselves off from the covenant.

19:2 "Be holy, for I, the Lord, your God, am holy." This is the first rule of conduct in the life of holiness—to recognize God as the source of life. If we wish to live we must keep God's order. Holiness is of primary importance because God is first of all holy. In God, holiness (wholeness) and oneness are the same. We speak of the one, holy God. The secret to a full (holy) life is found in the Code of Holiness. The order is so simple that we are apt to overlook the meaning of command.

The order in God is perfect, since there is only one God. The oneness of God is a mystery, and in oneness there is no room for disorder. This monotheistic conception of life and the source of life in the world and in the history of the Israelite people is traced to the revelation to Moses in Exod 3:14: "I am who am." The divine drawing out of one leader (Moses) and one people (Israel) reflects a new monotheistic way of thinking. God is drawing out of the people the life of God present in their midst, in their very living. As the people were held in slavery, so the life of God in the people was held captive. The command to be holy completes the circle by drawing out and returning life to the source of life. "I am who am" is God's way of saying "I am the source of life."

Order is heaven's first law. The proper order comes first. The "One" comes first. God is the only One who can say "I am who am." So God comes first

LORD, am your God.

⁴"Do not turn aside to idols, nor make molten gods for yourselves. I, the LORD, am your God.

⁵"When you sacrifice your peace offering to the LORD, if you wish it to be acceptable, ⁶it must be eaten on the very day of your sacrifice or on the following day. Whatever is left over until the third day shall be burned up in the fire. ⁷If any of it is eaten on the third day, the sacrifice will be unacceptable as refuse; ⁸whoever eats of it then shall pay the penalty for having profaned what is

and the Book of Leviticus records the proper order. To be holy because God is holy is to accept God as the source of life.

In Lev 19:3 the next command in order is reverence for parents, since through them we come into covenant contact with God, the source of life. This is why reverence for parents and keeping the sabbath are joined together in the text. Filial reverence recognizes parents as the contact point with the reality of life and the Creator of the whole of life.

Both parents and sabbath are joined for another reason. God rested on the seventh day and made it holy (Gen 2:3). The sabbath is, then, a holy day for the whole family. Celebration of the prime source of life will, in proper order, include the secondary source (parents). The order cannot be reversed. There is a proper order to living the Lord's day. The regulation of the sabbath is, in its final analysis, the regulation of the tithe, which puts God first. The portion, one day in seven (the holy unity), is the tithe commanded by God (Lev 27:30).

19:4 "Do not turn aside to idols or make molten gods for yourselves." Note that the making of images is not forbidden, but to turn to molten gods or images used as objects of worship is forbidden. In fact, it is the Spirit of God who continues to move today in the creative talent of artists who try, in a particular ordering of creation, to express the image and likeness of God as the source of all life. In the Hebrew rendering of this rule of conduct (v. 4), there is a wordplay on "El," the name of the god of neighboring people (18:3). The same root word is used to express "dumb idols."

19:5-8 An acceptable peace offering. Peace is the tranquility of order. If order is kept, peace results. The peace offering should be eaten on the day it is offered or on the next day, but not on the third day for then it becomes refuse (unclean). One living the life of holiness profanes oneself by eating the three-day-old offering. The obvious reason, besides spoilage, is that order is not followed. It was directed that on the third day the remaining part was to be burned, not eaten. Recall that those peace offerings are better called welfare or well-being offerings. Thus the recognition of the source of life and the insurance of the well-being of the people are brought about by following the order. The very reason for the peace offering is to recognize the continuing presence of the divine as the source of life for the well-being of the people.

sacred to the LORD. Such a one shall be cut off from his people.

⁹"When you reap the harvest of your land, you shall not be so thorough that you reap the field to its very edge, nor shall you glean the stray ears of grain. ¹⁰Likewise, you shall not pick your vineyard bare, nor gather up the grapes that have fallen. These things you shall leave for the poor and the alien. I, the LORD, am your God.

¹¹"You shall not steal. You shall not lie or speak falsely to one another. ¹²You shall not swear falsely by my name, thus profaning the name of your God. I am the LORD.

¹³"You shall not defraud or rob your neighbor. You shall not withhold overnight the wages of your day laborer. ¹⁴You shall not curse the deaf, or put a stumbling block in front of the blind, but you shall fear your God. I am the LORD.

¹⁵"You shall not act dishonestly in rendering judgment. Show neither partiality to the weak nor deference to the mighty, but judge your fellow men justly. ¹⁶You shall not go about spread-

To partake of unclean food profanes the sacred presence of the One who is the vital part of the community.

19:9 Sharing the harvest. Next in the life-order are those lives threatened by a lack of food. Those who have food and are able to acknowledge the source of life through the peace offering (thanksgiving for well-being) are really unable to give authentic witness to a life in holiness (completeness of the community) as long as there are those in that community who are poor. The regulation in verse 9 was established to give the poor the chance to live. This allows God as the source of all life to be at work in the whole community. Completeness and wholeness are what the life of holiness is all about.

The same rule is true in regard to the vines. The people are commanded to leave the grapes that have fallen (v. 10). This is God's way of giving them to the poor and the stranger. But they are not to leave anything for the fertility gods in payment for the crop, as was the custom of the land. "I am the source of all life; I, the Lord, am your God."

This latter exclamation is repeated several times in chapters 18 and 19. It appears that these chapters are a unit; perhaps they are the very first gathering of the materials into a manual of holiness. The exclamation "I, the Lord, am your God" is a clear reference to the first commandment of the Sinai Covenant Code and draws attention to the one God as the source of life. This recognition comes first in order (Exod 20:2-6; Lev 26:45). The repetition of the exclamation could have been used as a memory aid for the original manual. It could also mean that there were neighboring unacceptable practices (Lev 18:3; 20:23) well known to them at the time, and the frequent pauses in the text would make room for a litany-like response of short oaths of allegiance. The exclamation is the beginning of the first commandment. The community would continue, then, to publicly acclaim God, the Holy One, as the source of life.

ing slander among your kinsmen; nor shall you stand by idly when your neighbor's life is at stake. I am the LORD.

¹⁷"You shall not bear hatred for your brother in your heart. Though you may have to reprove your fellow man, do not incur sin because of him. ¹⁸Take no revenge and cherish no grudge against your fellow countrymen. You shall love your neighbor as yourself. I am the LORD.

¹⁹"Keep my statutes: do not breed any of your domestic animals with others of a different species; do not sow a field of yours with two different kinds of seed; and do not put on a garment woven with two different kinds of thread.

²⁰"If a man has carnal relations with a female slave who has already been living with another man but has not yet been redeemed or given her freedom, they shall be punished but not put to death,

19:16 "You shall not stand by idly when your neighbor's life is at stake." This regulation is joined to the command to avoid slander. No wonder, since the phrase used for slander means "to cut someone down by the spoken word." One can either stand in the way, stand by idly, or stand up to support the life at stake in one's neighbor. A witness to the truth can be an assertion of God as the source of life. In every circumstance we are obliged to weigh properly the life of our neighbor in the scale of justice. Therefore, if we accept the life of holiness we cannot stand by idly when falsehood is parading in the guise of truth for the destruction of life.

19:17, 18 "You shall love your neighbor as yourself." This and 19:2, "Be holy for I, the LORD your God, am holy," are the most quoted verses of Leviticus. Later Jesus will join these two together in answering "Which commandment of the Torah is the greatest?" His answer will be "You shall love the Lord, your God with your *whole* heart, with your *whole* soul and with *all* your mind" (Matt 22:37 quoting Deut 6:5). "The second is like to it, You shall love your neighbor as yourself" (Matt 22:39 quoting Lev 19:18). If one is living the life of holiness, which is described by the use of *whole* and *all*, then, everyone is neighbor to each other in this life. However, there is a holy sequence. Love of God comes first and includes love of neighbor, but love of neighbor does not, of necessity, lead immediately to love of the Holy One.

In verse 19 certain mixtures are prohibited. In the attempt to reflect the oneness of God in the wholeness of community life, the Priestly writers list some disorderly arrangements: crossbreeding, sowing two different seeds (one atop the other), and the tension of incompatible threads. The result of crossbreeding can be monstrous; different seeds vie for the same ground and moisture; the purity of the fabric is lost and the unity of the weaving is gone.

19:20-22 Atonement for relations with a female slave. The affirmation of the one source of life and the reflection of this oneness in the community is of prime importance. Thus the seriousness of sexual disorder or disorder in the control of life (v. 20) is shown by the requirement of a ram guilt offer-

because she is not free. ²¹The man, moreover, shall bring to the entrance of the meeting tent a ram as his guilt offering to the Lord. ²²With this ram the priest shall make atonement before the Lord for the sin he has committed, and it will be forgiven him.

²³"When you come into the land and plant any fruit tree there, first look upon its fruit as if it were uncircumcised. For

ing in reparation. The importance of recognizing and affirming the source of life is deeper than meets the eye. For example, the slave girl does not have a life of her own since she is not free. Supposedly she would win her freedom if she were put to death (the creature's relationship with God goes beyond life and death), and the justice of Yahweh would be satisfied. The question at hand is not only that justice be done but also that the holiness of life be preserved. The man in this disorderly sexual relation also has a life of his own. Thus through the guilt offering he is forgiven his sin (v. 22). She then keeps her "non-status," death is not affirmed, and the man is purified for life in holiness. The proper order of recognition of God as the source of life is not disturbed. The sanctuary is also involved (v. 21), since the text is talking about sex as the sacred control of life. The ultimate support of life-control (sex) must be a proper orientation (order in worship) to God, the source of life.

The sex act of humans outside marriage is out of order. There is an order to the use of sex. The coming together of two people in the act of sex forms one body (Gen 2:24). It is the two that choose to act as one. This new oneness can result in the affirmation of existing life and creation of life. When God blesses man and woman in Gen 1:28 with the command "Be fertile and multiply," God is inviting them to a deeper share in the divine oneness, a share in the very power of the one source of life to create new life. It is this added dimension of oneness that must be affirmed before the couple engage in sexual union—a oneness that in turn can become a source of life here on earth. This new affirmation of God as the one source of life also affirms the true role of the couple in the covenant relationship. This affirmation is what the marriage covenant is all about.

In the case of the slave girl, it must be remembered that she is already living with a man (Lev 19:20). This could mean that the oneness of the Source of Life is already recognized and affirmed. The man who now has sexual union with her is definitely acting out of order. Sexual union among humans, then, has to do with the proper ordering or control of life. First, the oneness of God as the one source of life is affirmed, and then the oneness of the couple as a secondary source of life follows.

19:23-25 Uncircumcised fruit. Fruit trees take time to mature and first fruits cannot be given to the Lord until the fourth year. Then the first fruits can be given to the Lord for that year's harvest as a thanksgiving offering.

three years, while its fruit remains uncircumcised, it may not be eaten. ²⁴In the fourth year, however, all of its fruit shall be sacred to the LORD as a thanksgiving feast to him. ²⁵Not until the fifth year may you eat its fruit. Thus it will continue its yield for you. I, the LORD, am your God.

²⁶"Do not eat meat with the blood still in it. Do not practice divination or soothsaying. ²⁷Do not clip your hair at the temples, nor trim the edges of your beard. ²⁸Do not lacerate your bodies for the dead, and do not tattoo yourselves. I am the LORD.

²⁹"You shall not degrade your daughter by making a prostitute of her; else the land will become corrupt and full of lewdness. ³⁰Keep my sabbaths, and reverence my sanctuary. I am the LORD.

³¹"Do not go to mediums or consult fortune-tellers, for you will be defiled by them. I, the LORD, am your God.

³²"Stand up in the presence of the aged, and show respect for the old: thus shall you fear your God. I am the LORD.

³³"When an alien resides with you in your land, do not molest him. ³⁴You shall treat the alien who resides with you no differently than the natives born among you; have the same love for him as for yourself; for you too were once aliens in the land of Egypt. I, the LORD, am your God.

³⁵"Do not act dishonestly in using measures of length or weight or capacity. ³⁶You shall have a true scale and true weights, an honest ephah and an honest hin. I, the LORD, am your God, who brought you out of the land of Egypt. ³⁷Be careful, then, to observe all my statutes and decrees. I am the LORD."

20 **Penalties for Various Sins.** ¹The LORD said to Moses, ²"Tell the Israelites: Anyone, whether an Israelite or an alien residing in Israel, who gives any of his offspring to Molech shall be

As the rite of circumcision brought a Jewish male into life-relationship with the covenant, so the fruit had to be looked upon as uncircumcised (v. 23) until the fourth year, when it was brought into the covenant. Only in the fifth year could the fruit be eaten.

19:32 Respect for the elderly. The verse states that to stand up in the presence of the aged is a way to show respect. The length of life is a gift of the Lord; respect for the length of life is reverence for the God of life. In other words, we are not looking at the person as such. The criterion for respect is not the wealth the person has accumulated nor fame attained, but simply the length of years. The time that the life-power of the Creator has been at work in the world, in the individual, and in the community must be respected in the life of holiness.

20:1-21 Penalties for various sins. There are two groups of penalties here, corresponding to the twofold commandment of love of God and love of neighbor. In verses 1-8 violation of the holy name (the name of holiness) is treated. In verses 9-21 love of neighbor, starting with one's parents, is considered. The penalty for transgression is, of course, real or symbolic death. To be cut off and to be put to death seem to come together in the meaning and the extent of the penalty. The Code puts the recognition of God as the source of life at the head of the list. It follows that one who acts contrary

put to death. Let his fellow citizens stone him. ³I myself will turn against such a man and cut him off from the body of his people; for in giving his offspring to Molech, he has defiled my sanctuary and profaned my holy name. ⁴Even if his fellow citizens connive at such a man's crime of giving his offspring to Molech, and fail to put him to death, ⁵I myself will set my face against that man and his family and will cut off from their people both him and all who join him in his wanton worship of Molech. ⁶Should anyone turn to mediums and fortune-tellers and follow their wanton ways, I will turn against such a one and cut him off from his people. ⁷Sanctify yourselves, then, and be holy; for I, the

LORD, your God, am holy. ⁸Be careful, therefore, to observe what I, the LORD, who make you holy, have prescribed.

⁹"Anyone who curses his father or mother shall be put to death; since he has cursed his father or mother, he has forfeited his life. ¹⁰If a man commits adultery with his neighbor's wife, both the adulterer and the adulteress shall be put to death. ¹¹If a man disgraces his father by lying with his father's wife, both the man and his stepmother shall be put to death; they have forfeited their lives. ¹²If a man lies with his daughter-in-law, both of them shall be put to death; since they have committed an abhorrent deed, they have forfeited their

to the recognition is cut off from the whole of life; this is the meaning of death. To be holy means to be fully alive.

20:2 Capital punishment. Israel allowed capital punishment by stoning. It was carried out by the whole community. One who refused to recognize God as the source of life was cut off from the community and put to death by stoning. There is a reference here to Molech. The word is akin to the Hebrew word for king and may be a graphic way of explaining that God comes first. The sanctuary becomes defiled when the palace becomes the place of worship. If the king is put first, then the king becomes one's source of life. One is cut off from the life of the Holy One and is dead to life in holiness. If the king is called upon, Yahweh is not acknowledged as the source of life. God alone can say, "I am who am" (meaning of Yahweh). No wonder the Jews were disturbed when Jesus said, "I solemnly declare it: before Abraham came to be, I AM," and they picked up rocks to stone him (John 8:58, 59). The holy name is blasphemed in Lev 24:16, and the consequent punishment is stoning by the community. No longer is that person allowed to be a member of the community of people who are living the life of holiness.

20:9 Cursing one's parents. These penalties concern the regulations of chapters 17, 18, and 19. The sacredness of the parental relation heads the list. The other penalties concern the disorder of control of life (sexuality) and of relationships of family and neighbor. Cursing is making light of something. To not only refuse proper crediting but even to discredit the proper order is what convicts a person. One who curses his or her parents, forfeits life (v. 9). This, in turn, leaves little room for recognition of God as the direct source of life. Such a state results in death. One cannot cut off the source of life without experiencing death.

lives. ¹³If a man lies with a male as with a woman, both of them shall be put to death for their abominable deed; they have forfeited their lives. ¹⁴If a man marries a woman and her mother also, the man and the two women as well shall be burned to death for their shameful conduct, so that such shamefulness may not be found among you. ¹⁵If a man has carnal relations with an animal, the man shall be put to death, and the animal shall be slain. ¹⁶If a woman goes up to any animal to mate with it, the woman and the animal shall be slain; let them both be put to death; their lives are forfeit. ¹⁷If a man consummates marriage with his sister or his half-sister, they shall be publicly cut off from their people for this shameful deed; the man shall pay the penalty of having had intercourse with his own sister. ¹⁸If a man lies in sexual intercourse with a woman during her menstrual period, both of them shall be cut off from their people, because they have laid bare the flowing fountain of her blood. ¹⁹You shall not have intercourse with your mother's sister or your father's sister; whoever does so shall pay the penalty of incest.

²⁰If a man disgraces his uncle by having intercourse with his uncle's wife, the man and his aunt shall pay the penalty by dying childless. ²¹If a man marries his brother's wife and thus disgraces his brother, they shall be childless because of this incest.

²²"Be careful to observe all my statutes and all my decrees; otherwise the land where I am bringing you to dwell will vomit you out. ²³Do not conform, therefore, to the customs of the nations whom I am driving out of your way, because all these things that they have done have filled me with disgust for them. ²⁴But to you I have said: Their land shall be your possession, a land flowing with milk and honey. I am giving it to you as your own, I, the LORD, your God, who have set you apart from the other nations. ²⁵You, too, must set apart, then, the clean animals from the unclean, and the clean birds from the unclean, so that you may not be contaminated with the uncleanness of any beast or bird or of any swarming creature in the land that I have set apart for you. ²⁶To me, therefore, you shall be sacred; for I, the LORD, am sacred, I,

20:22-27 Land ownership. Identity is fixed when people have a place to call their own. God has set the land apart for the people, who are to set themselves apart from the customs of the neighbor (vv. 24, 26). They must recognize this order and actually bring it about by setting themselves apart, the clean from the unclean (20:25). Thus they assert the commanding position of Yahweh.

20:24 A land flowing with milk and honey. Exod 3:8 is referred to here. The secondary source of the milk is the cow, sheep, goat, or camel, but God is the primary source of the milk and of honey from bees (see Sir 39:26). Because of the scarcity of clean water, milk was their most important drink. The land of Canaan is *fat* or wealthy (one of the meanings of the Hebrew word for milk). It is truly a "land flowing with milk and honey." Bees were plentiful, and deposited honey in the crevices of rocks or in hollow trees, even in the wilderness. In verse 24 God is affirmed as the source of these life-sustaining foods.

In verses 1-21 the penalties for not recognizing relation with God and neighbor are listed. In verses 22-27 the proper order of obedience is iden-

who have set you apart from the other nations to be my own.

²⁷"A man or a woman who acts as a medium or fortune-teller shall be put to death by stoning; they have no one but themselves to blame for their death."

21 **Sanctity of the Priesthood.** ¹The LORD said to Moses, "Speak to Aaron's sons, the priests, and tell them: None of you shall make himself unclean for any dead person among his people, ²except for his nearest relatives, his mother or father, his son or daughter, his brother ³or his maiden sister, who is of his own family while she remains unmarried; for these he may make himself unclean. ⁴But for a sister who has married out of his family he shall not make himself unclean; this would be a profanation.

⁵"The priests shall not make bare the crown of the head, nor shave the edges of the beard, nor lacerate the body. ⁶To their God they shall be sacred, and not profane his name; since they offer up the oblations of the LORD, the food of their God, they must be holy.

⁷"A priest shall not marry a woman who has been a prostitute or has lost her honor, nor a woman who has been divorced by her husband; for the priest is sacred to his God. ⁸Honor him as sacred who offers up the food of your God; treat him as sacred, because I, the LORD, who have consecrated him, am sacred.

⁹"A priest's daughter who loses her honor by committing fornication and thereby dishonors her father also, shall be burned to death.

¹⁰"The most exalted of the priests, upon whose head the anointing oil has been poured and who has been ordained to wear the special vestments, shall not bare his head or rend his garments, ¹¹nor shall he go near any dead person. Not even for his father or mother may he thus become unclean ¹²or leave the sanctuary; otherwise he will profane the sanctuary of his God, for with the anointing oil upon him, he is dedicated to his God, to me, the LORD.

¹³"The priest shall marry a virgin. ¹⁴Not a widow or a woman who has been divorced or a woman who has lost her honor as a prostitute, but a virgin, taken from his own people, shall he marry; ¹⁵otherwise he will have base offspring among his people. I, the LORD, have made him sacred."

Irregularities. ¹⁶The LORD said to Moses, ¹⁷"Speak to Aaron and tell him: None of your descendants, of whatever generation, who has any defect shall come forward to offer up the food of his God. ¹⁸Therefore, he who has any of the following defects may not come forward: he who is blind, or lame, or who has any disfigurement or malformation, ¹⁹or a crippled foot or hand, ²⁰or who is humpbacked or weakly or walleyed, or

---

tified. Through obedience both God and people maintain an identity which is founded on covenant faith, not on fortune-telling (20:27).

Chs. 21–22 Mediators, sacrificial banquets, and sacrificial victims. The identities of God and people have been established. For God the identity is in the ordering. For the people their identity is in the obedient response. It is appropriate to consider now the mediators of these covenant relations: Moses who directs the priesthood (21:1-24) and the victim of the sacrifice (22:17-33). The irregularities concerning priest and victim find a certain balanced presentation in the text. Many regulations required for the state of purification are restated in relation to the priest and the victim. These considerations act as an introduction for what is to come in chapter 23. Moses is still the mediator. His role might best be described as the lawgiver-high priest. He is the one to direct and guide Aaron's sons, the priests (21:1).

who is afflicted with eczema, ringworm or hernia. ²¹No descendant of Aaron the priest who has any such defect may draw near to offer up the oblations of the Lord; on account of his defect he may not draw near to offer up the food of his God. ²²He may, however, partake of the food of his God: of what is most sacred as well as of what is sacred. ²³Only, he may not approach the veil nor go up to the altar on account of his defect; he shall not profane these things that are sacred to me, for it is I, the LORD, who make them sacred."

²⁴Moses, therefore, told this to Aaron and his sons and to all the Israelites.

22 **Sacrificial Banquets.** ¹The LORD said to Moses, ²"Tell Aaron and his sons to respect the sacred offerings which the Israelites consecrate to me; else they will profane my holy name. I am the LORD.

³"Tell them: If any one of you, or of your descendants in any future generation, dares, while he is in a state of uncleanness, to draw near the sacred offerings which the Israelites consecrate to the LORD, such a one shall be cut off from my presence. I am the LORD.

⁴"No descendant of Aaron who is stricken with leprosy, or who suffers from a flow, may eat of these sacred offerings, unless he again becomes clean. Moreover, if anyone touches a person who has become unclean by contact with a corpse, or if anyone has had an emission of seed, ⁵or if anyone touches any swarming creature or any man whose uncleanness, of whatever kind it may be, is contagious, ⁶the one who touches such as these shall be unclean until evening and may not eat of the sacred portions until he has first bathed

his body in water; ⁷then, when the sun sets, he again becomes clean. Only then may he eat of the sacred offerings, which are his food. ⁸He shall not make himself unclean by eating of any animal that has died of itself or has been killed by wild beasts. I am the LORD.

⁹"They shall keep my charge and not do wrong in this matter; else they will die for their profanation. I am the LORD who have consecrated them.

¹⁰"Neither a lay person nor a priest's tenant or hired servant may eat of any sacred offering. ¹¹But a slave whom a priest acquires by purchase or who is born in his house may eat of his food. ¹²A priest's daughter who is married to a layman may not eat of the sacred contributions. ¹³But if a priest's daughter is widowed or divorced and, having no children, returns to her father's house, she may then eat of her father's food as in her youth. No layman, however, may eat of it. ¹⁴If such a one eats of a sacred offering through inadvertence, he shall make restitution to the priest for the sacred offering, with an increment of one fifth of the amount. ¹⁵The sacred offerings which the Israelites contribute to the LORD the priests shall not allow to be profaned ¹⁶nor in the eating of the sacred offering shall they bring down guilt that must be punished; it is I, the LORD, who make them sacred."

Unacceptable Victims. ¹⁷The LORD said to Moses, ¹⁸"Speak to Aaron and his sons and to all the Israelites, and tell them: When anyone of the house of Israel, or any alien residing in Israel, who wishes to offer a sacrifice, brings a holocaust as a votive offering or as a free-will offering to the LORD, ¹⁹if it is to be acceptable, the ox or sheep or goat

The irregularities of chapters 21:2–22:33, especially those of 21:16 ff., may seem strange to us, but we must remember that today we know a great deal more about many of these maladies than did the biblical people. At that time, some irregularites were simply considered punishment from God. Judgments of impurity and profanation were often based on the person's inability to perform a particular action, as in the case of blind, crippled, and disfigured individuals.

that he offers must be an unblemished male. ²⁰You shall not offer one that has any defect, for such a one would not be acceptable for you. ²¹When anyone presents a peace offering to the LORD from the herd or the flock in fulfillment of a vow, or as a free-will offering, if it is to find acceptance, it must be unblemished; it shall not have any defect. ²²One that is blind or crippled or maimed, or one that has a running sore or mange or ringworm, you shall not offer to the LORD; do not put such an animal on the altar as an oblation to the LORD. ²³An ox or a sheep that is in any way ill-proportioned or stunted you may indeed present as a free-will offering, but it will not be acceptable as a votive offering. ²⁴One that has its testicles bruised or crushed or torn out or cut off you shall not offer to the LORD. You shall neither do this in your own land ²⁵nor receive from a foreigner any such animals to offer up as the food of your God; since they are deformed or defective, they will not be acceptable for you."

²⁶The LORD said to Moses, ²⁷"When an ox or a lamb or a goat is born, it shall remain with its mother for seven days;

only from the eighth day onward will it be acceptable, to be offered as an oblation to the LORD. ²⁸You shall not slaughter an ox or a sheep on one and the same day with its young. ²⁹Whenever you offer a thanksgiving sacrifice to the LORD, so offer it that it may be acceptable for you; ³⁰it must, therefore, be eaten on the same day; none of it shall be left over until the next day. I am the LORD.

³¹"Be careful to observe the commandments which I, the LORD, give you, ³²and do not profane my holy name; in the midst of the Israelites I, the LORD, must be held as sacred. It is I who made you sacred ³³and led you out of the land of Egypt, that I, the LORD, might be your God."

23 **Holy Days.** ¹The LORD said to Moses, ²"Speak to the Israelites and tell them: The following are the festivals of the LORD, my feast days, which you shall celebrate with a sacred assembly.

³"For six days work may be done; but the seventh day is the sabbath rest, a day for sacred assembly, on which you shall do no work. The sabbath shall belong to the LORD wherever you dwell.

Chapter 23 has a beauty all its own. It describes the life of holiness in terms of the feasts of Israel. The list begins with the sabbath rest (23:3). By keeping a day of complete rest God is recognized as the source of the life of holiness (Gen 2:3). The list continues with mention of Passover, Pentecost, New Year's day, the Day of Atonement, and finally the third pilgrim feast, the feast of Booths. The order in which these are presented is significant. The purpose of Leviticus is not to give a detailed instruction for festival observance but to draw attention to the need for these celebrations in order to give recognition to God's plan of life. "I am the Lord, your God," must be repeated every six days. The holy number was seven; thus the seventh day became the Lord's day. The seventh day represents the tithe of time that belongs to God.

23:1-44 Holy days. Throughout the Pentateuch there are calendars of holy days (Exod 23:14-18; 34:18-25; Lev 23; Deut 16:1-16). In Leviticus the three pilgrim feasts are mentioned: Passover-Unleavened Bread (23:4-14); the feast of Weeks or Pentecost (23:15-22); and the feast of Booths (23:33-44). New Year's day (vv. 23-25) and the Day of Atonement (vv. 26-32) are added.

Passover. 4"These, then, are the festivals of the LORD which you shall celebrate at their proper time with a sacred assembly. 5The Passover of the LORD falls on the fourteenth day of the first month, at the evening twilight. 6The fifteenth day of this month is the LORD's feast of Unleavened Bread. For seven days you shall eat unleavened bread. 7On the first of these days you shall hold a sacred assembly and do no sort of work. 8On each of the seven days you shall offer an oblation to the LORD. Then on the seventh day you shall again hold a sacred assembly and do no sort of work.

9The LORD said to Moses, 10"Speak to the Israelites and tell them: When you come into the land which I am giving you, and reap your harvest, you shall bring a sheaf of the first fruits of your harvest to the priest, 11who shall wave the sheaf before the LORD that it may be acceptable for you. On the day after the sabbath the priest shall do this. 12On this day, when your sheaf is waved, you shall offer to the LORD for a holocaust an unblemished yearling lamb. 13Its cereal offering shall be two tenths of an ephah of fine flour mixed with oil, as a sweet-smelling oblation to the LORD; and its libation shall be a fourth of a hin of wine. 14Until this day, when you bring your God this offering, you shall not eat any bread or roasted grain or fresh kernels. This shall be a perpetual statute for you and your descendants wherever you dwell.

Pentecost. 15"Beginning with the day after the sabbath, the day on which you bring the wave-offering sheaf, you shall count seven full weeks, 16and then on the day after the seventh week, the fiftieth day, you shall present the new cereal offering to the LORD. 17For the wave offering of your first fruits to the LORD, you shall bring with you from wherever you live two loaves of bread

The sabbath heads the list (v. 3). God made the sabbath holy (Gen. 2:3; see Exod 20:8-11 and Heb 4:4, 9). The listing is merely an announcement on the part of Moses (Lev 23:44). As long as one is a covenant member, every day is holy. Certain days, however, are designated by God, through Moses, to be celebrated with a holy assembly (23:1-3).

In ancient stories of other peoples, the sacred assembly took place among the gods. With Israel the Holy One initiates the gathering of the people (Lev 23:4; Exod 12:16). By gathering the major feasts into one place (in the Levitical material of the Pentateuch), the Priestly writers affirm the mediatorship of Moses in the celebrations of the people.

The order in which the list appears gives the reader a mosaic of the life of holiness in the world—the Holy One living in the midst of the people. The feast of Passover-Unleavened Bread celebrates freedom from slavery. Fifty days later, the end of the harvest and the offering of the first fruits begins with the celebration of Weeks (Pentecost). Then, there is one final look back at the wilderness with the feast of Booths, which commemorates the booth made from branches and the tent dwelling of the wanderings in the wilderness. It was also called the feast of Tabernacles, and since it was celebrated at the end of harvest time it received the name of Ingathering. Throughout this description of life, the beginning of each year is announced at a celebration, and every year the whole of life rejoices in the Day of Atonement.

made of two tenths of an ephah of fine flour and baked with leaven. ¹⁸Besides the bread, you shall offer to the LORD a holocaust of seven unblemished yearling lambs, one young bull, and two rams, along with their cereal offering and libations, as a sweet-smelling oblation to the LORD. ¹⁹One male goat shall be sacrificed as a sin offering, and two yearling lambs as a peace offering. ²⁰The priest shall wave the bread of the first fruits and the two lambs as a wave offering before the LORD; these shall be sacred to the LORD and belong to the priest. ²¹On this same day you shall by proclamation have a sacred assembly, and no sort of work may be done. This shall be a perpetual statute for you and your descendants wherever you dwell.

²²"When you reap the harvest of your land, you shall not be so thorough that you reap the field to its very edge, nor shall you glean the stray ears of your grain. These things you shall leave for the poor and the alien. I, the LORD, am your God."

New Year's Day. ²³The LORD said to Moses, ²⁴"Tell the Israelites: On the first day of the seventh month you shall keep a sabbath rest, with a sacred assembly and with the trumpet blasts as a reminder; ²⁵you shall then do no sort of work, and you shall offer an oblation to the LORD."

The Day of Atonement. ²⁶The LORD said to Moses, ²⁷"The tenth of this seventh month is the Day of Atonement, when you shall hold a sacred assembly and mortify yourselves and offer an oblation to the LORD. ²⁸On this day you shall not do any work, because it is the Day of Atonement, when atonement is made for you before the LORD, your God. ²⁹Anyone who does not mortify himself on this day shall be cut off from his people; ³⁰and if anyone does any work on this day, I will remove him from the midst of his people. ³¹This is a perpetual statute for you and your descendants wherever you dwell: you shall do no work, ³²but shall keep a sabbath of complete rest and mortify yourselves. Beginning on the evening of the ninth of the month, you shall keep this sabbath of yours from evening to evening."

The Feast of Booths. ³³The LORD said to Moses, ³⁴"Tell the Israelites: The fifteenth day of this seventh month is the LORD's feast of Booths, which shall continue for seven days. ³⁵On the first day there shall be a sacred assembly, and you shall do no sort of work. ³⁶For seven days you shall offer an oblation to the LORD, and on the eighth day you shall again hold a sacred assembly and offer an oblation to the LORD. On that solemn closing you shall do no sort of work.

³⁷"These, therefore, are the festivals of the LORD on which you shall proclaim a sacred assembly, and offer as an oblation to the LORD holocausts and cereal offerings, sacrifices and libations, as prescribed for each day, ³⁸in addition to those of the LORD's sabbaths, your dona-

The feast of Booths is mentioned at the end of the list. Its many names and its accent on dwelling show a development in its significance. No wonder that later Peter will want permission to erect three booths, one for Moses the lawgiver, one for Elijah the prophet, and one for Jesus the life-giver.

Chapters 23–25 should probably be read as a unit, since they speak of holy days, holy places and holy land. The days are holy (23:1-44) and the sanctuary lamp (24:1-4) and showbread (24:5-9) point to the holy meeting place. The sabbatical year (25:1-7) and the jubilee year (25:8-22) with redemption of property (25:23-55) deal with the holy land (25:1-22), property rights (25:23-38), and freedom (25:39-55). Chapter 23 describes the life of holiness with emphasis on the presence of the Holy One living in the midst of the

tions, your various votive offerings and the free-will offerings that you present to the LORD.

³⁹"On the fifteenth day, then, of the seventh month, when you have gathered in the produce of the land, you shall celebrate a pilgrim feast of the LORD for a whole week. The first and the eighth day shall be days of complete rest. ⁴⁰On the first day you shall gather foliage from majestic trees, branches of palms and boughs of myrtles and of valley poplars, and then for a week you shall make merry before the LORD, your God. ⁴¹By perpetual statute for you and your descendants you shall keep this pilgrim feast of the LORD for one whole week in the seventh month of the year. ⁴²During this week every native Israelite among

you shall dwell in booths, ⁴³that your descendants may realize that, when I led the Israelites out of the land of Egypt, I made them dwell in booths. I, the LORD, am your God."

⁴⁴Thus did Moses announce to the Israelites the festivals of the LORD.

24 The Sanctuary Light. ¹The LORD said to Moses, ²"Order the Israelites to bring you clear oil of crushed olives for the light, so that you may keep lamps burning regularly. ³In the meeting tent, outside the veil that hangs in front of the commandments, Aaron shall set up the lamps to burn before the LORD regularly, from evening till morning. Thus, by a perpetual statute for you and your descendants, ⁴the lamps shall be set up on the pure

people, whereas the sabbatical and jubilee celebrations of chapter 25, with their note of perfection in the holy number seven, seem to be looking beyond this life to the life of perfect holiness in God (the eternal Holy of Holies). Every seven years the whole land has a complete rest as a sabbath for the Lord (25:2-4). Then, in the jubilee life of perfection (seven times seven weeks of years), all shall return to their property (25:10,13). But the Lord does not have a role in redemption of the land as the sanctuary had a role in purification (ch. 16) because God is the source of life and the owner of the land (25:23). Recall that God actually dwelt only in the cloud above the propitiatory seat of mercy in 16:2.

24:1-4 The sanctuary lamp. This repeats the regulations in Exod 27:20, 21. Exodus closes with Moses putting the lampstand in the meeting tent and arranging the bread on the table before the Lord (40:22-40). So now, at the close of Leviticus, the lamp and the table of display are arranged in the proper Levitical order. Here, however, the emphasis is not on the pure oil as in Exod 27, but on the presence of the Holy. (This is much like the symbolism of the tabernacle light in churches today.) When there is a light in the window, there is somebody home. So, the Holy One and the people who are to be holy are at home in the one covenant. The showbread, or the bread of display, represents the people (Lev 24:5-9), with six loaves in each of two piles on a small table. The piles are a reminder of the twelve tribes, like the two onyx memorial stones with the engraved tribal names as part of the priest's vestments (Exod 28:9-12). Thus, the Holy One and the people are present to each other by real signs of life. The oil is replenished (Lev 24:2) and the bread is kept fresh (24:8). For a life of holiness it is necessary to have

gold lampstand, to burn regularly before the LORD.

The Showbread. ⁵"You shall take fine flour and bake it into twelve cakes, using two tenths of an ephah of flour for each cake. ⁶These you shall place in two piles, six in each pile, on the pure gold table before the LORD. ⁷On each pile put some pure frankincense, which shall serve as an oblation to the LORD, a token offering for the bread. ⁸Regularly on each sabbath day this bread shall be set out afresh before the LORD, offered on the part of the Israelites by an everlasting agreement. ⁹It shall belong to Aaron and his sons, who must eat it in a sacred place, since, as something most sacred among the various oblations to the LORD, it is his by perpetual right."

Punishment of Blasphemy. ¹⁰Among the Israelites there was a man born of an Israelite mother (Shelomith, daughter of Dibri, of the tribe of Dan) and an Egyptian father. ¹¹This man quarreled publicly with another Israelite and cursed and blasphemed the LORD's name. So the people brought him to Moses, ¹²who kept him in custody till a decision from the LORD should settle the case for them. ¹³The LORD then said to Moses, ¹⁴"Take the blasphemer outside the camp, and when all who heard him have laid their hands on his head, let the whole community stone him. ¹⁵Tell the Israelites: Anyone who curses his God shall bear the penalty of his sin; ¹⁶whoever blasphemes the name of the LORD shall be put to death. The whole community shall stone him; alien and native alike must be put to death for blaspheming the LORD's name.

¹⁷"Whoever takes the life of any human being shall be put to death; ¹⁸whoever takes the life of an animal shall make restitution of another animal. A life for a life! ¹⁹Anyone who inflicts an

an ongoing experience of the presence of each other—of the Holy One and the people who are to be holy.

24:10-23 Punishment for blasphemy and murder. What is holy can become profaned (the light is snuffed out when it should be burning) or the people can become defiled (the bread becomes unclean, stale). However, means will be given to affirm both the holy and the people or to redeem them from profanity or defilement (see ch. 25). In this life of holiness there is no atonement/redemption that can be made for the blasphemer (24:16) or for the murderer (Num 35:31). The reasoning is thus: the Hebrew word for blasphemy suggests a piercing, in some way, of the name of the Holy One. Piercing could bring about the flow of the lifeblood of the victim as in the case of murder. The life of God is in the Holy Name and the life of the human is in the blood, so by blasphemy and by murder, both God and human are pierced. The blasphemer and the murderer must be put to death.

There is also a wordplay in the text on the name Shelomith (24:10), a name similar to that of a neighboring goddess who was considered complete, holy. Such a substitution for the Holy One of Israel would be a blasphemy. The punishment for this violation would be stoning and consequent cutting off such an offender from the covenant of the life of holiness.

It is important to note that the text maintains the covenant arrangement (24:23). Moses is asked what to do about the blasphemer, but God is the Holy One who gives the command for the blasphemer to be cut off from

injury on his neighbor shall receive the same in return. ²⁰Limb for limb, eye for eye, tooth for tooth! The same injury that a man gives another shall be inflicted on him in return. ²¹Whoever slays an animal shall make restitution, but whoever slays a man shall be put to death. ²²You shall have but one rule, for alien and native alike. I, the LORD, am your God."

²³When Moses told this to the Israelites, they took the blasphemer outside the camp and stoned him; they carried out the command that the LORD had given Moses.

25 **The Sabbatical Year.** ¹The LORD said to Moses on Mount Sinai, ²"Speak to the Israelites and tell them: When you enter the land that I am giving you, let the land, too, keep a sabbath for the LORD. ³For six years you may sow your field, and for six years prune your vineyard, gathering in their produce. ⁴But during the seventh year the land shall have a complete rest, a sabbath for the LORD, when you may neither sow your field nor prune your vineyard. ⁵The aftergrowth of your harvest you shall not reap, nor shall you pick the grapes of your untrimmed vines in this

the life of holiness (v. 14). Those who heard the blasphemy must join in, since they received the profanation through their ears. They are joined together in the life of the Holy One. By the laying on of their hands, they return the blasphemy to the offender and by stoning send it to death, a place of no return (24:14).

In chapter 25 the focus is on atonement, not in the sense of forgiveness but in the sense of at-one-ment, union resulting from full acceptance of the covenant relationship. The orderly arrangement of the Priestly material continues in these final chapters.

We can now see the atonement (ch. 16) effected in and reflected by the life of holiness (chs. 17–26). The celebration of the holy days (ch. 23) brings atonement for a more complete living (ch. 25) with the rewards and punishments attached to obedience or disobedience to the Code of Holiness (ch. 26). The two members of the covenant are reidentified and reaffirmed (ch. 24). Chapter 27 becomes another bridge-chapter but, unlike chapter 16, this bridge is only partially constructed.

25:1-22 Sabbatical and jubilee years. During the seventh year the land shall have a complete rest (25:4), a sabbath for the Lord. Even the land is holy and, as the Lord set aside the seventh day, so the land is affirmed as holy in the seventh year. In the seventh month of the forty-ninth year and continuing into the fiftieth year, the celebration is called jubilee, "the year of the ram's horn." We think of jubilation. On this Atonement Day the horn is blown to call the sacred assembly. The word for horn also has the meaning of removing the veil to see the beauty of the woman or to see the clear blue sky when the cloud is gone. Chapter 25:10 says, "You shall make sacred this fiftieth year, by proclaiming liberty in the land for all its inhabitants. It shall be a jubilee for you."

year of sabbath rest for the land. ⁶While the land has its sabbath, all its produce will be food equally for you yourself and for your male and female slaves, for your hired help and the tenants who live with you, ⁷and likewise for your livestock and for the wild animals on your land.

The Jubilee Year. ⁸"Seven weeks of years shall you count—seven times seven years—so that the seven cycles amount to forty-nine years. ⁹Then, on the tenth day of the seventh month let the trumpet resound; on this, the Day of Atonement, the trumpet blast shall re-echo throughout your land. ¹⁰This fiftieth year you shall make sacred by proclaiming liberty in the land for all its inhabitants. It shall be a jubilee for you, when every one of you shall return to his own property, every one to his own family estate. ¹¹In this fiftieth year, your year of jubilee, you shall not sow, nor shall you reap the aftergrowth or pick the grapes from the untrimmed vines. ¹²Since this is the jubilee, which shall be sacred for you, you may not eat of its produce, except as taken directly from the field.

¹³"In this year of jubilee, then, every one of you shall return to his own property. ¹⁴Therefore, when you sell any land to your neighbor or buy any from him, do not deal unfairly. ¹⁵On the basis of the number of years since the last jubilee shall you purchase the land from him; and so also, on the basis of the number of years for crops, shall he sell it to you. ¹⁶When the years are many, the price shall be so much the more; when the years are few, the price shall be so much the less. For it is really the number

The people are free and return to their families (25:10). There is no more sowing or reaping (v. 11). If they obey, their dwelling is secure (not movable as in the wilderness, v. 18). The land will yield its fruit. They will have food in abundance so that they may live without worry (v. 19). There will be crops for three years, and even in the ninth year they will eat from the old planting because the eternal covenant in the life of holiness has begun.

In 24:17-21 we saw the legal aspect of the Code of Holiness in what is usually referred to as the law of retaliation or recompense—an eye for an eye, a tooth for a tooth, a life for a life, etc. Each of three Codes in the Torah mentions this human balance of justice (Exod 21:24; Lev 24:17-21, and Deut 19:21). As we continue in the Code, we begin to experience the justice of God at one with an unconditional love. A certain holiness begins to enter into real-life situations, given unconditionally by God. A certain stability and wholeness of every life relationship comes to those who, in obedience, recognize the one, holy God as the source of life and live according to the Code.

We are not dealing here with just memories or vain hopes. These are moral directives that give beat and pulse to real living. They are life-support dynamics of the celebration of the wholeness (holiness) of life. They are the vertebrae of the divine-human covenant. Slavery and exile are still the human condition of unfaithful covenant partners, but the enduring and sustaining presence of the Holy One is at work in the midst of the people (Lev 26:44, 45).

of crops that he sells you. ¹⁷Do not deal unfairly, then; but stand in fear of your God. I, the LORD, am your God.

¹⁸"Observe my precepts and be careful to keep my regulations, for then you will dwell securely in the land. ¹⁹The land will yield its fruit and you will have food in abundance, so that you may live there without worry. ²⁰Therefore, do not say, 'What shall we eat in the seventh year, if we do not then sow or reap our crop?' ²¹I will bestow such blessings on you in the sixth year that there will then be crop enough for three years. ²²When you sow in the eighth year, you will continue to eat from the old crop; and even into the ninth year, when the crop comes in, you will still have the old to eat from.

Redemption of Property. ²³"The land shall not be sold in perpetuity; for the land is mine, and you are but aliens who have become my tenants. ²⁴Therefore, in every part of the country that you occupy, you must permit the land to be redeemed. ²⁵When one of your countrymen is reduced to poverty and has to sell some of his property, his closest relative, who has the right to redeem it, may go and buy back what his kinsman has sold. ²⁶If, however, the man has no relative to redeem his land, but later on acquires sufficient means to buy it back in his own name, ²⁷he shall make a deduction from the price in proportion to the number of years since the sale, and then pay back the balance to the one to whom he sold it, so that he may thus regain his own property. ²⁸But if he does not acquire sufficient means to buy back his land, what he has sold shall remain in the possession of the purchaser until the jubilee, when it must be released and returned to its original owner.

²⁹"When someone sells a dwelling in a walled town, he has the right to buy it back during the time of one full year from its sale. ³⁰But if such a house in a walled town has not been redeemed at the end of a full year, it shall belong in perpetuity to the purchaser and his

This is as far as the Book of Leviticus takes us in the Torah of the Holy One.

Some commentators refer to these later sections as a portrayal of an ideal life. This is true but the life of holiness was never meant to remain just an ideal. When the Torah was given, with Leviticus as its heart, the world received the plan of living a holy life.

The final form of the holiness begins to take shape. The remaining pieces will fall readily into place. This chapter in the five-volume work of the Law is about to complete its message.

Before we consider the partially constructed bridge (ch. 27), we need to look at a final note about the redemption of property in chapter 25 and the material in chapter 26, which was the standard way of closing a covenant treaty.

25:23-55 Redemption of property. The perfect (holy) calendar is presented in the first part of chapter 25, followed by the sacred activity of the holy jubilation year (vv. 23-55). The intended results of the Code were to be: Yahweh recognized as king (vv. 23, 55); wealth redistributed every jubilee (vv. 6, 7); families (v. 10), the land (vv. 2-4), and everyone enjoying liberty (vv. 10, 54); the land bearing fruit (v. 19) of itself (v. 11); all debts canceled (vv. 36, 37); the poor lifted up (vv. 25, 35, 39, 47, 48)—everyone

descendants; nor shall it be released in the jubilee. ³¹However, houses in villages that are not encircled by walls shall be considered as belonging to the surrounding farm land; they may be redeemed at any time, and in the jubilee they must be released.

³²In levitical cities the Levites shall always have the right to redeem the town houses that are their property. ³³Any town house of the Levites in their cities that had been sold and not redeemed, shall be released in the jubilee; for the town houses of the Levites are their hereditary property in the midst of the Israelites. ³⁴Moreover, the pastureland belonging to their cities shall not be sold at all; it must always remain their hereditary property.

³⁵When one of your fellow countrymen is reduced to poverty and is unable to hold out beside you, extend to him the privileges of an alien or a tenant, so that he may continue to live with you. ³⁶Do not exact interest from your countryman either in money or in kind, but out of fear of God let him live with you. ³⁷You are to lend him neither money at interest nor food at a profit. ³⁸I, the LORD, am your God, who brought you out of the land of Egypt to give you the land of Canaan and to be your God.

³⁹When, then, your countryman becomes so impoverished beside you that he sells you his services, do not make him work as a slave. ⁴⁰Rather, let him be like a hired servant or like your tenant, working with you until the jubilee year, ⁴¹when he, together with his children, shall be released from your service and return to his kindred and to the property of his ancestors. ⁴²Since those whom I

and everything whole in the life of holiness. Note that the land remains the possession of the Holy One. "The land shall not be sold in perpetuity; for the land is mine, and you are but aliens who have become my tenants." (Later you may become my children but, for now you are my renters.) "Therefore, in every part of the country you occupy, you must permit the land to be redeemed" (vv. 23, 24). That is, if they live in the life of holiness, they must acknowledge Yahweh as the original owner, the source of life.

Yahweh had already ordered and taken part in the cleansing and purification of the sanctuary, the meeting tent and the altar, as well as the priests and all the people of the community (16:20, 33). Now a further order is given. Unlike the negative order in Gen 2:17 (see also Gen 3:22), "From that tree you shall not eat," there is the positive command to share in the life of holiness: "Be holy."

While we cannot with certainty sort out the various traditions woven together in Leviticus, we can see changing conditions in the story and can come to some conclusions as to its message at the time of the final editing. For example, walled cities and open-air villages are provided for here, and throughout Leviticus the traveling tabernacle is given emphasis. Such references suggest different chronological times in Israel's development. Yet, behind these observations and the ordered structure of the regulations and directives we see the truth of Lev 25:23: God is the owner of land and property; the people are but aliens who have become tenants.

25:25 Redemption of property. After recognizing that Yahweh owns the

brought out of the land of Egypt are servants of mine, they shall be sold as slaves to any man. ⁴³Do not lord it over them harshly, but stand in fear of your God.

⁴⁴"Slaves, male and female, you may indeed possess, provided you buy them from among the neighboring nations. ⁴⁵You may also buy them from among the aliens who reside with you and from their children who are born and reared in your land. Such slaves you may own as chattels, ⁴⁶and leave to your sons as their hereditary property, making them perpetual slaves. But you shall not lord it harshly over any of the Israelites, your kinsmen.

⁴⁷"When one of your countrymen is reduced to such poverty that he sells himself to a wealthy alien who has a permanent or a temporary residence among you, or to one of the descendants of an immigrant family, ⁴⁸even after he has thus sold his services he still has the right of redemption; he may be redeemed by one of his own brothers, ⁴⁹or by his uncle or cousin, or by some other relative or fellow clansman; or, if he acquires the means, he may redeem himself. ⁵⁰With his purchaser he shall compute the years from the sale to the jubilee, distributing the sale price over these years as though he had been hired as a day laborer. ⁵¹The more such years there are, the more of the sale price he shall pay back as ransom; ⁵²the fewer years there are left before the jubilee year, the more he has to his credit; in proportion to his years of service shall he pay his ransom. ⁵³The alien shall treat him as a servant hired on an annual basis, and he shall not lord it over him harshly under your very eyes. ⁵⁴If he is not thus redeemed, he shall nevertheless be released, together with his children, in the jubilee year. ⁵⁵For to me the Israelites belong as servants; they are servants of mine, because I brought them out of the land of Egypt, I, the LORD, your God.

26 **The Reward of Obedience.** ¹"Do not make false gods for yourselves. You shall not erect an idol or a sacred pillar for yourselves, nor shall you set up a stone figure for worship in your land; for I, the LORD, am your God. ²Keep my sabbaths, and reverence my sanctuary. I am the LORD.

land and the property, the poor come first and this for the good of the family (vv. 23-28). As we read verses 23-55, it is as though the owner is preparing to buy back the dwelling in the midst of the people in the wilderness. Chapter 27 will expand this idea of the plan of redemption. Chapter 26 seems to say, "Take your choice, but there is only one correct choice if you want to live the life of holiness. If you choose obedience or disobedience, here are the respective consequences!"

26:3-13 "Live in accord with my precepts." If one gives obedience to these precepts of the life of holiness and the commandments (actually the Code of Holiness in chapter 19 includes the commandments of the Sinai Code in Exod 20), then all kinds of life-giving experiences will happen (vv. 3-13). "If you obey, I will set my Dwelling among you, and will not disdain you" (vv. 11-13).

26:14-46 Punishment for disobedience. If the community members are unfaithful, terrible things will happen (vv. 16, 17). If they still disobey, terrible things will happen to the world in which they live (vv. 19, 20). If they become defiant, things will get worse by seven times (each time in vv. 18, 21, 24,

³"If you live in accordance with my precepts and are careful to observe my commandments, ⁴I will give you rain in due season, so that the land will bear its crops, and the trees their fruit; ⁵your threshing will last till vintage time, and your vintage till the time for sowing, and you will have food to eat in abundance, so that you may dwell securely in your land. ⁶I will establish peace in the land, that you may lie down to rest without anxiety. I will rid the country of ravenous beasts, and keep the sword of war from sweeping across your land. ⁷You will rout your enemies and lay them low with your sword. ⁸Five of you will put a hundred of your foes to flight, and a hundred of you will chase ten thousand of them, till they are cut down by your sword. ⁹I will look with favor upon you, and make you fruitful and numerous, as I carry out my covenant with you. ¹⁰So much of the old crops will you have stored up for food that you will have to discard them to make room for the new. ¹¹I will set my Dwelling among you, and will not disdain you. ¹²Ever present in your midst, I will be your God, and you will be my people; ¹³for it is I, the LORD, your God, who brought you out of the land of the Egyptians and freed you from their slavery, breaking the yoke they had laid upon you and letting you walk erect.

Punishment of Disobedience. ¹⁴"But if you do not heed me and do not keep all these commandments, ¹⁵if you reject my precepts and spurn my decrees, refusing to obey all my commandments and breaking my covenant, ¹⁶then I, in turn, will give you your deserts. I will punish you with terrible woes — with wasting and fever to dim the eyes and sap the life. You will sow your seed in vain, for your enemies will consume the crop. ¹⁷I will turn against you, till you are beaten down before your enemies and lorded over by your foes. You will take to flight though no one pursues you.

¹⁸"If even after this you do not obey me, I will increase the chastisement for your sins sevenfold, ¹⁹to break your haughty confidence. I will make the sky above you as hard as iron, and your soil as hard as bronze, ²⁰so that your

and 28 punishment is increased seven times over), until they will be forced to eat their own children (v. 29). This dire situation could happen in order to survive the siege of walled cities. In their defiant struggle to survive, they themselves would revoke the results (children) of their covenant with the Source of Life. A complete breakdown in the relations of God and people with the whole of life being overturned in death and exile (vv. 30-33) would occur.

26:34 The land shall retrieve its lost sabbaths. This is the built-in payment plan put there by God. While the people are in exile, the land rests. Everything comes to a standstill. The sabbaths must be kept and the precepts followed by the people, even though unwillingly. Sabbath payments are made to God and the people can do nothing about it. Verse 36 returns to the threat of verse 17. Finally, when "their uncircumcised hearts are humbled and they make amends" (v. 41), God will start over with the people. God is holy and remembers the covenant made with their ancestors (v. 42). Exile actually gives the land and the people time to rest (v. 43). The land became defiled when the people defiled themselves by their disobedience. Now both lie desolate,

strength will be spent in vain; your land will bear no crops, and its trees no fruit.

21"If then you become defiant in your unwillingness to obey me, I will multiply my blows another sevenfold, as your sins deserve. 22I will unleash the wild beasts against you, to rob you of your children and wipe out your livestock, till your population dwindles away and your roads become deserted.

23"If, with all this, you still refuse to be chastened by me and continue to defy me, 24I, too, will defy you and will smite you for your sins seven times harder than before. 25I will make the sword, the avenger of my covenant, sweep over you. Though you then huddle together in your walled cities, I will send in pestilence among you, till you are forced to surrender to the enemy. 26And as I cut off your supply of bread, ten women will need but one oven for baking all the bread they dole out to you in rations—not enough food to still your hunger.

27"If, despite all this, you still persist in disobeying and defying me, 28I, also, will meet you with fiery defiance and will chastise you with sevenfold fiercer punishment for your sins, 29till you begin to eat the flesh of your own sons and daughters. 30I will demolish your high places, overthrow your incense stands, and cast your corpses on those of your idols. In my abhorrence of you, 31I will lay waste your cities and devastate your sanctuaries, refusing to accept your sweet-smelling offerings. 32So devastated will I leave the land that your very enemies who come to live there will stand aghast at the sight of it. 33You yourselves I will scatter among the nations at the point of my drawn sword, leaving your countryside desolate and your cities deserted. 34Then shall the land retrieve its lost sabbaths during all the time it lies waste, while you are in the land of your enemies; then shall the land have rest and make up for its sabbaths 35during all the time that it lies desolate, enjoying the rest that you would not let it have on the sabbaths when you lived there.

36"Those of you who survive in the lands of their enemies I will make so fainthearted that, if leaves rustle behind them, they will flee headlong, as if from the sword, though no one pursues them; 37stumbling over one another as if to escape a weapon, while no one is after them—so helpless will you be to take a stand against your foes! 38You will be lost among the Gentiles, swallowed up in your enemies' country. 39Those of you who survive in the lands of their enemies will waste away for their own and their fathers' guilt.

40"Thus they will have to confess that they and their fathers were guilty of having rebelled against me and of having defied me, 41so that I, too, had to defy them and bring them into their enemies' land. Then, when their uncircumcised

in reprieve for the land and in punishment for the people (v. 43), until time has elapsed equal to the sabbaths defiled. The land is holy because it also belongs to the Lord (25:23). Whenever the land is defiled (polluted), it lies desolate.

God's love is unconditional, since the Holy One does not allow the covenant to be voided, even though God is the only faithful one remaining (vv. 44, 45). This unconditional love is under, behind, and all around the Torah Law. The Book of Leviticus has now become the heart inserted into the Torah and, with its lively beat of the Code of Holiness, the People of God find themselves invited again to share in the life of the Holy One.

hearts are humbled and they make amends for their guilt, ⁴²I will remember my covenant with Jacob, my covenant with Isaac, and my covenant with Abraham; and of the land, too, I will be mindful. ⁴³But the land must first be rid of them, that in its desolation it may make up its lost sabbaths, and that they, too, may make good the debt of their guilt for having spurned my precepts and abhorred my statutes. ⁴⁴Yet even so, even while they are in their enemies' land, I will not reject or spurn them, lest, by wiping them out, I make void my covenant with them; for I, the Lord, am their God. ⁴⁵I will remember them because of the covenant I made with their forefathers, whom I brought out of the land of Egypt under the very eyes of the Gentiles, that I, the Lord, might be their God."

⁴⁶These are the precepts, decrees and laws which the Lord had Moses promul-

gate on Mount Sinai in the pact between himself and the Israelites.

V: REDEMPTION OF OFFERINGS

27 **Redemption of Votive Offerings.** ¹The Lord said to Moses, ²"Speak to the Israelites and tell them: When anyone fulfills a vow of offering one or more persons to the Lord, who are to be ransomed at a fixed sum of money, ³for persons between the ages of twenty and sixty, the fixed sum, in sanctuary shekels, shall be fifty silver shekels for a man, ⁴and thirty shekels for a woman; ⁵for persons between the ages of five and twenty, the fixed sum shall be twenty shekels for a youth, and ten for a maiden; ⁶for persons between the ages of one month and five years, the fixed sum shall be five silver shekels for a boy, and three for a girl; ⁷for persons of sixty or more, the fixed sum shall be fifteen

Throughout the reading of Leviticus, this simple outline has been stressed: obedience (chs. 1–27), purification (chs. 8–27) and holiness-sanctification (chs. 17–27). Obedience endures as a requirement. Obedience of the human partner of the covenant is requested by and made possible by God. The purification of the relationship reaches its anticlimax in the atonement chapter (Lev 16). Here the covenant partners meet and prepare for the climax of the covenant relationship in the life of holiness (Lev 27). Chapter 27 describes only the beginning of the perfect life, and for this reason is "an open-ended bridge-chapter." The perfect life of holiness is begun in the acceptance and practice of the Code of Holiness.

PART V: REDEMPTION OF VOTIVE OFFERINGS

Lev 27

It is understandable why many commentators treat this final chapter as an appendix to Leviticus. It gives the impression of an afterthought, added later because of its importance. The meaning of Lev 27 is so simple that it can be easily overlooked: It affirms God and people as faithful covenant partners. Its open-ended character suggests that the divine-human covenant is still in the stage of promise.

shekels for a man, and ten for a woman. [8]However, if the one who took the vow is too poor to meet the fixed sum, the person must be set before the priest, who shall determine the sum for his ransom in keeping with the means of the one who made the vow.

[9]"If the offering vowed to the LORD is an animal that may be sacrificed, every such animal, when vowed to the LORD, becomes sacred. [10]The offerer shall not present a substitute for it by exchanging either a better for a worse one or a worse for a better one. If he attempts to offer one animal in place of another, both the original and its substitute shall be treated as sacred. [11]If the animal vowed to the LORD is unclean and therefore unfit for sacrifice, it must be set before the priest, [12]who shall determine its value in keeping with its good or bad qualities, and the value set by the priest shall stand. [13]If the offerer wishes to redeem the animal, he shall pay one fifth more than this valuation.

[14]"When someone dedicates his house as sacred to the LORD, the priest shall determine its value in keeping with its good or bad points, and the value set by the priest shall stand. [15]If the one who dedicated his house wishes to redeem it, he shall pay one fifth more than the price thus established, and then it will again be his.

[16]"If the object which someone dedicates to the LORD is a piece of his heredi-

Some might be tempted to read into the text the fact that the Messiah-Redeemer had not as yet come as reason for the open-ended treatment. This would be an assumption beyond what is contained in Leviticus. The concentration is still upon God as creator of life and Moses as lawgiver-mediator presenting the rules of conduct of the Sinai Covenant. Leviticus has reaffirmed the Sinai Covenant in adding the new dimension of holiness in the sense of completeness. The people are now to become fully alive (holy).

The secret in understanding chapter 27 lies in the meaning of the vow and the tithe. It begins by vowing all of creation to God: persons (vv. 2-8); livestock (vv. 9-13); dwelling (vv. 14, 15); hereditary land (vv. 16-24). The chapter ends by returning everything to God in the tithe (vv. 26-34).

In the preceding chapter the divine partner of the covenant spelled out the results, good and bad, of the obedience or disobedience of the junior member. Here the Holy One respects the free will of the human partner and points the way of respect for the divine partner.

The practice of making a vow to a deity in order to receive a favor or cure is very ancient. However, we are dealing with a more basic idea: the holiness of life. The vow and its redemption, along with the practice of tithing, make possible the holy life. As a free-will offering, the vow affirms human life. The tithe affirms divine life.

In chapter 27 God affirms human free will and gives conditions whereby the votive offering can be redeemed. Everyone and everything in creation is considered. The meaning of vow goes to the very root of life. In a way every vow to God is a promise to live a holy life. God wills the creature

tary land, its valuation shall be made according to the amount of seed required to sow it, the acreage sown with a homer of barley seed being valued at fifty silver shekels. ¹⁷If the dedication of a field is made at the beginning of a jubilee period, the full valuation shall hold; ¹⁸but if it is some time after this, the priest shall estimate its money value according to the number of years left until the next jubilee year, with a corresponding rebate on the valuation. ¹⁹If the one who dedicated his field wishes to redeem it, he shall pay one fifth more than the price thus established, and so reclaim it. ²⁰If, instead of redeeming such a field, he sells it to someone else, it may no longer be redeemed; ²¹but at the jubilee it shall be released as sacred to the LORD; like a field that is doomed, it shall become priestly property.

²²"If the field that some man dedicates to the LORD is one he had purchased and not a part of his hereditary property, ²³the priest shall compute its value in proportion to the number of years until the next jubilee, and on the same day the price thus established shall be given as sacred to the LORD; ²⁴at the jubilee, however, the field shall revert to the hereditary owner of this land from whom it had been purchased.

²⁵"Every valuation shall be made according to the standard of the sanctuary shekel. There are twenty gerahs to the shekel.

Offerings Not To Be Redeemed. ²⁶"Note that a first-born animal, which as such already belongs to the LORD, may not be dedicated by vow to him. If it is an ox or a sheep, it shall be ceded to the LORD; ²⁷but if it is an unclean animal, it may be redeemed by paying one fifth more than its fixed value. If it is not redeemed, it shall be sold at its fixed value.

²⁸"Note, also, that any one of his possessions which a man vows as doomed to the LORD, whether it is a human being or an animal or a hereditary field, shall be neither sold nor ransomed; everything that is thus doomed becomes most sacred to the LORD. ²⁹All human beings that are doomed lose the right to be redeemed; they must be put to death.

to be fully alive, that is, holy. In Gen 1:26, 27 the creature is created in the image and likeness of God, able to assert its own freedom. The buying back of life in all of creation must be done according to God's terms. The priest sets the price, but the terms are according to the rules of the jubilee, God's life-giving celebration (vv. 17, 18, 21, 23, 24). God, then, remains the source of life and holiness.

Certain offerings cannot be redeemed: the first-born and, at the other end of life, those doomed to die (vv. 26-29). They affirm God as the ultimate source of life. There is a refinement here of the dedication of Exod 13. Every first-born that opens the womb among the Israelites, both of man and beast, belongs to the Lord. It cannot be the object of a vow (dependent on human free will). It still acts as a reminder of the death of the first-born of the Egyptians, who would not recognize Yahweh as the source of life (Exod 13:14-16). Death is still the human condition (Gen 3:19), but now the emphasis is on dedication and redemption.

27:28-29 "All human beings that are doomed." The Hebrew word for "doomed" in verse 28 also has the meaning of "dedicated," that is, "set aside

30"All tithes of the land, whether in grain from the fields or in fruit from the trees, belong to the LORD, as sacred to him. 31If someone wishes to buy back any of his tithes, he shall pay one fifth more than their value. 32The tithes of the herd and the flock shall be determined by ceding to the LORD as sacred every tenth animal as they are counted by the herdsman's rod. 33It shall not matter whether good ones or bad ones are thus chosen, and no exchange may be made. If any exchange is attempted, both the original animal and its substitute shall be treated as sacred, without the right of being bought back."

34These are the commandments which the LORD gave Moses on Mount Sinai for the Israelites.

for the Lord." God alone has control over the human being, animal, or land that has become most sacred (dedicated). In modern-day parallel, people on death row are doomed to die, but appeal can be made to the highest authority. Another meaning of the word is "people dedicated by solemn vow to God." In the order of holiness they are on "life's row." It is the will of the divine covenant member that all live. Life, not death, is the will of God. Death came into the world because of the *human* covenant member (Gen 3), and death is still present to the community of the human covenant members. However, the divine partner could play the role of the lesser member and then restore life to the human condition.

27:30-33 The sacredness of tithes. The above explanation is only partial. In an unfinished bridge-chapter we expect some partial answers. As in Gen 28, the vow and the tithe are now brought together in chapter 27 to affirm and ensure the continued presence of God. The tithe becomes the span of the bridge that we set in place, even though constructed of material belonging to the Lord.

We need to rethink our definition of tithe. We are not speaking of one-tenth as of multiples of ten. In the creation of the world, the tithe was the seventh day. Each of the six days of creation is made up of the created things of the previous day plus its own works. The seventh day was made holy (Gen 1:3). The seventh day in the creation blueprint became a miniature world, holy and complete, a fitting expression of the creator's gift of the world. The Lord's day is a holy day. It is the original form of the tithe. "Seventh" and "complete rest" are from the same Hebrew root word. The seventh day is the day of completion.

Deut 14:22-29 puts the finishing touches on the understanding of tithing. "Each year you shall tithe all . . . then in the place which the Lord, your God, chooses as the dwelling place of his name you shall eat in his presence your tithe . . . . that you may learn always to fear [respect the source of life] the Lord, your God" (14:22-23). In verse 26, after making provision for everyone, Deuteronomy directs all to partake of the tithe and make merry with their families.

Deuteronomy continues the regulation "at the end of every third year, you shall bring all the tithes . . . for that year and deposit them in community stores, that the Levite . . . the alien, the orphan and the widow . . . may come and eat their fill" (14:28-29). Let everyone enjoy fully the life of holiness.

The payment of the tithe is in the eating of the meal together (the Holy One and the ones called to be holy) with the feeding of the poor so that all may have life to the full. This is the life of holiness, a life that is being lived today in the Eucharist-Passover, the celebration of the redemption of the Firstborn. Gathered with the writers of the Book of Leviticus on the partially constructed bridge to the Dwelling of the Holy Name, we begin to hear the song of celebration: "Holy, holy, holy is the Lord of hosts! All the earth is filled with God's glory!"

REVIEW AIDS AND DISCUSSION TOPICS

I

Introduction (pages 5–12)

1. Define these terms: Torah, Leviticus, Pentateuch, Third Book of Moses. How do the Hebrew and the Latinized Greek names of the book help us understand Leviticus and its place in the Torah? How does the book point to Moses as the mediator of the covenant between God and Israel? Where is this indicated in the first chapter?

2. Discuss the example of the heart as a description of the position of Leviticus in the whole body of the Law. What section is described as the "heartbeat" of the Torah?

3. Why would "instruction" be a more appropriate translation of Torah than "law"?

4. Explain the meaning of holy in the Torah.

5. What are some ways in which Western and Near Eastern thought patterns differ? What effect does this have on the writing and reading of the Bible?

II

1:1–7:38 Ritual of Sacrifice (pages 15–29)

1. Discuss the order in these first seven chapters. Look at number 9 of the Introduction and notice the reading assignments and how material is divided. What texts indicate that the first three chapters are a unit.

2. What is a covenant? What makes a covenant different from an ordinary contract? What is the meaning of "the salt of the covenant?"

3. Discuss the various God-people relationships and their effect upon the entire community. In the Hebrew way of thinking, what happened to the community when a priest sinned or was found to be ritually unclean? How is the penalty paid to the Lord in the guilt offering?

4. Who usually made the atonement for the sin, and what was usually done with any offering that was left over? Explain the difference between sin offering and guilt offering.

5. Mention a guiding principle in the formation of a regulation.

6. What is meant by "being cut off from the people"? How is it related to covenant holiness?

7. In these first chapters (1–7) what is expected of the people? Is this an essential element in a covenant treaty?

8. For what did ritual obedience prepare (see chapters 11–16)?

III

8:1–10:20 Ceremony of Ordination (pages 29–35)

1. Why does this seem to be an ideal place to introduce the material concerning the dedication of the tabernacle/temple and the ordination of the priest? Discuss

the function of the priest. What is the difference today between the ordained priest and the priesthood of the laity?

2. In the ordination ceremony, what kind of offering was made for seven days? Why?

IV

11:1–16:34 Laws Regarding Legal Purity (pages 35–52)

1. Just as chapters 1–7 prepared for the purification of chapters 11–16, for what phase in the covenant relationship do these chapters prepare?

2. Why do we single out chapter 16? What term describes the purifying function of this chapter?

3. What is ritual impurity and the uncleanness of childbirth? Why did the menstrual flow make one unclean?

4. Why is a spring or a cistern considered pure?

5. Give three explanations of "outside the camp." Why is it necessary for the priest to go outside the camp to judge the condition of leprosy?

6. In "sprinkle seven times," what does sprinkle remind one of? Why "seven times"?

7. Why is blood touched to the tip of one's ear, thumb, and toe in the purification ceremony?

8. What two-fold process is included in the meaning of "cleanness"?

9. What is the propitiatory on the ark? Where did God actually dwell?

10. In the atonement rite why are two goats chosen? What ceremony signifies the passing over of blessing or sin? Recall other incidents of passing over.

11. Why, during the atonement rite, does the priest change vestments a number of times and after each change take a bath?

V

17:1–26:46 Code of Legal Holiness (pages 52–81)

1. Why does the Code of Holiness appeal to the reader more than what has gone before? What is the importance of the preceding chapters?

2. What two commandments of the Code of Conduct are repeated and quoted more than any other Bible phrases (chapter 19)? In the quotation that Jesus uses from Deuteronomy (Deut 6:5–Matt 22:37), what words emphasize the holiness of the command?

3. Give the simple threefold division of Leviticus (three words) and describe the contents of this book.

4. If putting the blood on the altar signified that God is the source of life, how was this signified when it was no longer possible for people to go to the temple?

5. What verse in chapter 18 shows that there is no room for divorce in the proper ordering of the life of holiness? What name do we give to this verse and why?

6. What is the first rule in the order of holiness? What follows after the first rule of conduct? In the second rule of conduct, why is the sabbath obligation joined

with the reverence for father and mother? In the order of celebration, where does the sabbatical obligation come (see chapters 23 and 25)? What is *seder*?

7. What do we mean when we say that "I, the Lord, am your God" is like a mini-oath?

8. Why does the cursing of a parent violate the recognition of God as the source of life? How does blasphemy against the name of the Holy One act like murder against a neighbor? What is the basic meaning of cursing?

9. How do the sanctuary lamp and the showbread represent the presence of the two covenant members? Why the two piles of six loaves? What makes the lamp oil and the bread "living signs?"

10. Give two reasons for the regulation of eating the peace offering on the second day, but not on the third day. What does this offering celebrate in the life of holiness?

11. By standing to respect the aged, what or who is actually being affirmed as the distinguished member of the covenant?

12. What is the reason for the prohibition (chapter 25) of the perpetual sale of land? How does the land retrieve its lost sabbaths?

13. If God took part in the purification of the sanctuary (chapter 16), why does God not speak of buying back the dwelling place of the divine presence in the redemption of property in chapter 25?

VI

27:1-34 Redemption of Votive Offerings (pages 81–85)

1. Discuss chapter 16 as a bridge between the descriptions of purification and holiness. Discuss chapter 27 as an unfinished bridge-chapter. How do the first and second parts of verse 18 act as a bridge to the two sections of chapter 18?

2. What is the meaning of "tithe"?

3. Would a fitting conclusion to the study of the Book of Leviticus be to plan a seder meal, with special attention to its ritual and to the questions asked during the meal?

4. For further study of the theme of holiness in the New Testament, read the First Letter of Peter and the Epistle to the Hebrews.